Analyzing Bar Charts for Profit

Analyzing Bar Charts for Profit

By
John Magee
Richard J. McDermott

Published By John Magee Inc.
Boston, Massachusetts

ISBN: 0-910944-03-2

Printed in the United States of America

Table of Contents

Chapter	Page
Acknowledgement	vii
Foreword	ix
1. Basic Tenets of Technical Analysis Evolved from Dow Jones Theory	1
2. Support and Resistance	6
3. Bar Charts and Their Uses	9
4. The Importance of Trends	40
5. Trend Channels	72
6. Gaps	74
7. The Magee Method	83
8. Selected Market Letters of John Magee (1982–1988)	86
Glossary	181
Glossary of Patterns	210
Index	219

Listing of Charts

Chart Number		**Page**
Chart A	Eagle Picher Industries	44
Chart B	Advanced Micro Devices Inc.	50
Chart C	B.F. Goodrich Company	52
Chart D	BankAmerica Corporation	54
Chart E	Arvin Industries	56
Chart F	Fedders USA Inc.	58
Chart G	COMDISCO Inc.	59
Chart H	AMAX Inc.	60
Chart I	Gap Incorporated	63
Chart J	Bally Manufacturing Corporation	64
Chart K	American Brands, Inc.	65
Chart L	Dillard Department Stores Inc.	67
Chart M	Cray Research Inc.	70
Chart N	MGIC Investment	77
Chart O	Consolidated Edison	80

Listing of Magee Market Letters

Letter		**Page**
January 23, 1982	Long-Term Chart, Your Long-Term Friend	87
May 22, 1982	The Shapes Behind the Shadows	89
May 29, 1982	Just One More Time...	91
June 5, 1982	Managing Money	93
August 21, 1982	Buying Panic (And What It Means)	95
September 4, 1982	Dangerous Spikes	97
February 19, 1983	Reflections	99
March 12, 1983	We Follow the Tape Not the Tube	101
March 19, 1983	Second Phase Stocks: Some Technical Observations	103
April 2, 1983	New Issues, High Technology, Wonder Stocks, and the Like	105
May 7, 1983	Beyond the Limits	107
June 25, 1983	Even a Stopped Clock Is Right Twice a Day	109
October 29, 1983	Jumping the Gun	111
November 12, 1983	A Prevalent Pattern	113
December 3, 1983	The Reason(s) for the Move	115

Letter		Page

March 10, 1984	Media Wonders	117
May 19, 1984	Drifters	119
September 1, 1984	Big Money in Brain Surgery: Learn at Home this Quick, Easy Way	121
September 22, 1984	Forecasting: No Such Thing as a Sure Thing	123
October 13, 1984	Which Way the Market: And Why	125
October 27, 1984	Calling the Turn: A Case of Missing the Point	127
November 17, 1984	Subject to Delay	129
November 24, 1984	On Protecting One's Assets	131
December 15, 1984	The Elliott Wave Theory: Perspective and Comments . . .	133
March 16, 1985	When a Stock Collapses: Crisis or Opportunity?	135
March 23, 1985	Acquisitions Fever Revisited	137
April 27, 1985	An Easy Way to Buy a Pile of Trouble	139
July 6, 1985	The First Shoe Drops	141
July 13, 1985	Protecting Stock Market Profits or a Trip into the Wild Blue Yonder and Back	143
September 14, 1985	The Hemline Barometer and Other "Mood" Measures as Crystal Balls to the Future	145
September 28, 1985	An Oversold Market	147
December 7, 1985	...And How High Do You Think It Will Go?	149
December 14, 1985	The Stock Market: Not So Random	151

Letter		Page

January 11, 1986	Professional Obsolescence	153
February 1, 1986	We Would Not Want to Get Scared Out of the Market Too Soon	155
February 22, 1986	Hole in One	157
July 12, 1986	Up Trendline Review	159
July 19, 1986	Head-and-Shoulders: A Continuing Tradition	161
November 8, 1986	The Rounding Turn—A Bird Worth Catching	163
December 20, 1986	Flags, Triangles and River Sediment	165
January 17, 1987	Big Blue—From Bellwether to Bust!	167
January 24, 1987	The Elusive Crystal Ball	169
June 6, 1987	Earnings Forecasts: Dangerous to Your Financial Health!	171
July 4, 1987	How Far Will It Go?	173
December 12, 1987	Wedge Review—A Bearish Tale	175
June 25, 1988	IBM Versus Dow Jones Averages	177
July 16, 1988	Currency Swings	179

Listing of Chart Patterns

Major Bullish (Bottoming) Patterns

Triple Bottom 211
Fan 211
Head-and-Shoulders Bottom (Simple) 211
Head-and-Shoulders Bottom (Complex) 211
One-Day Reversal 212
Island Reversal 212
Rounding Bottom (Bowl/Saucer) 212
Dormant Bottom 212

Major Bearish (Topping) Patterns

Triple Top 213
Fan 213
Head-and-Shoulders Top (Simple) 213
Head-and-Shoulders Top (Complex) 213
One-Day Reversal 214
Island Reversal 214
Rounding Top (Inverted Bowl) 214
Broadening Top 214

Indeterminant Patterns

Rectangle 215
Diamond 215
Triangle (Symmetrical) 215

Major Continuation Patterns (Of Previous Trend)

Head-and-Shoulders Consolidation 216
Pennant 216
Flag 216
Wedge (Rising) 216

Measurement Patterns

Flag 217
Triangle (Symmetrical) 217
Rectangle 218
Head-and-Shoulders Bottom 218

Acknowledgement

This book is dedicated to Gene R. Morgan, who has done more to promote technical analysis than anyone I know with the exception of John Magee.

Mr. Morgan has presented a live, daily, 30-minute television show called "Charting the Market" on KWHY, Channel 22, in Los Angeles for 28 years. He also lectures frequently at investor symposiums throughout California.

Richard McDermott
November, 1994

Foreword

THE EVOLUTION OF TECHNICAL ANALYSIS

About eighty years ago, in Springfield, Massachusetts, there lived a man named Charles H. Dow. He was one of the editors of a great newspaper, the *Springfield Republican*. When he left Springfield, it was to establish another great newspaper, the *Wall Street Journal*.

Charles Dow also laid the foundation for a new approach to market problems.

In 1884, he made up an average of the daily closing prices of eleven important stocks, nine of which were rails, and recorded the fluctuations of this average.

He believed that the judgment of the investing public, as reflected in the movements of stock prices, represented an evaluation of the future probabilities affecting the various industries. He saw in his average, a tool for predicting business conditions many months ahead. This was true because those who bought and sold these stocks included men intimately acquainted with the industrial situation from every angle. Dow reasoned that the price of a security, as determined by a free competitive market, represented the composite knowledge and appraisal of everyone interested in that security—financiers, officers of the company, investors, employees, customers— everyone, in fact, who might be buying or selling stock.

Dow felt that this market evaluation was probably the shrewdest appraisal of conditions to come that could be contained, since it integrated all known facts, estimates, surmises, and the hopes and fears of all interested parties.

It was William Peter Hamilton who really put these ideas to work. In his book, *The Stock Market Barometer*, published in

1922, he laid the ground work for the much-used and much-abused Dow Theory.

Unfortunately, a great many superficial students of the market never understood the original premises of the "barometer" and seized on the bare bones of the theory as a sort of magic touchstone to fame and easy fortune.

Others, discovering that the "barometer" was not perfect, set about devising corrections. They tinkered with the rules of classic Dow Theory, trying to find the wonderful formula that would avoid its periodic disappointments and failures.

Of course, what they forgot was that the averages were *only averages* at best. There is nothing very wrong with the Dow Theory. What is wrong is the attempt to find a simple universal formula—a set of measurements that will make a suit to fit every man, fat, thin, tall or short.

During the 1920s and 1930s, Richard W. Schabacker reopened the subject of technical analysis in a somewhat new direction. Schabacker, who had been financial editor of *Forbes Magazine*, set out to find some new answers. He realized that whatever significant action appeared in the average must derive from similar action in some of the stocks making up the average.

In his books, *Stock Market Theory and Practice*, *Technical Market Analysis*, and *Stock Market Profits*, Schabacker showed how the "signals" that had been considered important by Dow theorists when they appeared in the averages, were also significant and had the same meanings when they turned up in the charts of individual stocks.

Others, too, had noted these technical patterns. But it was Schabacker who collated, organized, and systematized the technical method. Not only that, he also discovered new technical indications in the charts of stocks; indications of a type that would ordinarily be absorbed or smothered in the averages, and, hence, not visible or useful to Dow theorists.

In the final years of his life, Richard Schabacker was joined by his brother-in-law, Robert D. Edwards, who completed Schabacker's last book and carried forward the research in technical analysis.

Edwards, in turn, was joined in this work in 1942 by John Magee. Magee, an alumnus of the Massachusetts Institute of Technology, was well-oriented to the scientific and technical approach.

Edwards and Magee retraced the entire road, re-examining the Dow Theory and re-studying the technical discoveries of Schabacker.

Basically, the original findings were still good. But with additional history and experience, it was possible to correct some details of earlier studies. Also, a number of new applications and methods were brought to light. The entire process of technical evaluation became more scientific.

It became possible to state more precisely, the premises of technical analysis. That the market represents a most democratic and representative criterion of stock values. That the action of a stock in a free, competitive market reflects all that is known, believed, surmised, hoped or feared about that stock, and, therefore, that it synthesizes the attitudes and opinions of all. That the price of the stock is the result of buying and selling forces and represents the "true value" at any given moment. That a Major Trend must be presumed to continue in effect until clear evidence of Reversal is shown. And, finally, that it is possible to form opinions having a reasonably high probability of confirmation from the market action of a stock as shown in daily, weekly, or monthly charts, or from other technical studies derived from the market activity of the security.

It is important to point out that the ultimate value of a security to the investor or trader is what he ultimately receives from it. That is to say, the price he gets when he sells it, or the market price he could obtain for it at any particular time, adjusted for dividends or capital distribution in either case. If, for example, he has bought a stock at $25 a share, and it has paid him $5 in dividends and is now bid at $35, he has a realized an accrued benefit of $5 plus $10, or $15 in all. It is the combination of dividends and appreciation of capital that constitutes his total gain.

It seems futile to try to correlate or compare the market value of a stock with the "book value," or with any "value" figured on a basis of capitalized earnings or dividends, projected growth, etc. There are too many other factors which may also affect the value, and some of these cannot easily be expressed in simple ratios. For example, a struggle for control of a corporation can as surely increase the value of its securities in the market as a growth of earnings. Again, a company may lose money for years and pay no dividends, yet still be an excellent investment on the basis of its development of potential resources as perceived by those who are buying and selling its stock. For the market is not evaluating *last year's* accomplishments as such, it is weighing the prospects for the year to come.

Then, too, in a time of inflation, a majority of stocks may advance sharply in price. This may reflect a depreciation in the purchasing power of dollars more than improvement in business conditions—but it is important, nonetheless, in such a case to be "out of" dollars and "into" equities.

As a result of their research from 1942 to 1948, Edwards and Magee developed new technical methods. They put these methods to practical use in actual market operation. And, eventually, in 1948, these findings were published in their definitive book, *Technical Analysis of Stock Trends.*

This book, now in its sixth edition, has become the accepted authority in this field. It has been used as a textbook by various schools and colleges, and is the basic tool of many investors and traders.

In 1951, Edwards retired from his work as a stock analyst, and John Magee continued the research, at first, independently, and then, from January, 1953 to March, 1956, as chief technical analyst with an investment counselling firm.

Meanwhile, beginning in 1950, Magee started on a new road, which, as it turned out, was destined to open up virgin fields of technical market research.

Using the methods of Dow, Hamilton, Schabacker, and Edwards as a base, he initiated a series of studies intended to discover new technical devices. These investigations were long and laborious, and, often they were fruitless. One study required four months of work, involved hundreds of sheets of tabulations, many thousands of computations—and proved nothing.

But from his type of work, eventually, in late 1951 there began to emerge some important new and useful concepts— new bricks to build into the structure of the technical method.

The new devices are not revolutionary. They do not vitiate the basic technical approach. Rather, they are evolutionary and add something to the valuable kit of tools already at hand. The new studies often make it possible to interpret and predict difficult situations *sooner and more dependably* than any other method previously used.

Mr. Magee has designated these newest technical devices the Delta Studies. They are basically an extension and refinement of the technical method. There is no magic in the Delta Studies. They do not provide infallible formulas for sure profits at all times in every transaction, but they have proved eminently successful over a period of years in practical use in actual market operations, as auxiliary to the methods outlined in the book, *Technical Analysis of Stock Trends*.

Through his technical work, John Magee emphasized these three principles:

1. Stock prices tend to move in trends;

2. Volume goes with the trends; and

3. A trend, once established, tends to continue in force.

A large portion of the book, *Technical Analysis of Stock Trends*, is devoted to the patterns which tend to develop when a trend is being reversed. Head-and-Shoulders, Tops and Bottoms, W-Patterns, Triangles, Rectangles, etc., are common patterns to stock market technicians. Rounding Bottoms and Drooping Necklines, are some of the more esoteric ones.

Magee urged investors to go with the trend, rather than trying to pick a Bottom before it was completed, or averaging down in a declining stock. Above all, and at all times, he refused to get involved in the game of forecasting where "the market" was headed, or where the DJIA would be on December 31st of the coming year. Rather, he preached care in individual stock selection regardless of which way the market "appeared" headed. Finally, his service recommended short positions as regularly as it did long positions, based simply on what the charts said.

To the random walker, who once confronted Magee with the statement that there is no predictable behavior in Wall Street, Magee's reply was classic. He said:

"You fellows rely too heavily on your computers. The best computer ever designed is still the human brain. Theoreticians try to simulate stock market behavior, and, failing to do so with any degree of predictability, declare that a journey through the stock market is a random walk. Isn't it equally possible that the programs simply aren't sensitive enough, or the computers strong enough, to successfully simulate the thought process of the human brain?"

Then Magee would walk over to his bin of charts, pull out a favorite, and show it to the random walker. There it was: spike up, heavy volume; consolidation, light volume; spike up again, heavy volume. And a third time and a fourth time. A beautifully symmetric chart, moving ahead in a well-defined trend channel, volume moving with the price.

"Do you really believe that these patterns are random?" Magee would ask, already knowing the answer.

We all have a favorite passage or quotation by our favorite author. My favorite quotation of John Magee's appears in the short booklet he wrote especially for subscribers to his technical Stock Advisory Service.

"When you enter the stock market you are going into a competitive field in which your evaluations and opinions will be matched against some of the sharpest and toughest minds in business. You are in a highly specialized industry in which there are many different sectors, all of which are under intense study by men whose economic survival depends upon their best judgment.

"You will most certainly be exposed to advice, suggestions, offers of help from all sides. And, unless you are able to develop some market philosophy of your own, you will not be able to tell the good from the bad, the sound from the unsound."

I doubt if any man alive has helped more investors develop a sound philosophy of investing in Wall Street than John Magee.

Analyzing Bar Charts for Profit originally appeared in the *Encyclopedia of Technical Analysis* as "Bar Charts for Decision-making." John Magee called it a discussion, we call it a monograph. He never intended it to be a book, but we thought it was such a concise explanation of the technical process of "pattern recognition" of bar charts that his followers would like to read it.

Richard McDermott
Editor and Revisor
Analyzing Bar Charts for Profit
President, John Magee, Inc.
November, 1994

For a detailed study of the technical method, the reader is referred to the definitive work on this subject, the book *Technical Analysis of Stock Trends* by Robert D. Edwards and John Magee.

This Book may be ordered directly from John Magee, Inc., 154 West Hubbard Street, Suite 304, Chicago, Illinois 60610 or by calling 1-800-595-9890. Fax orders may be sent to 312-595-9878.

Chapter 1:
Basic Tenets of Technical Analysis Evolved from Dow Jones Theory

John Magee's objective has always been to forecast *individual stock* prices—not the "overall" stock market. Investors buy *individual* stocks, not the "market"—their profits (or losses) reflect how well those stocks do. While it is often the case that the vast majority of stocks move in the same direction as the market, it is not always so. Certain groups may lead a market move, while others may lag or not participate at all. And, even within a group of stocks such as Airlines or Steel, for example, certain stocks may move ahead of, with, or actually lag behind their own group.

The basic tenets of technical analysis were first put forth by Charles Dow, editor of the *Wall Street Journal* and creator of the Dow Jones Averages. By analyzing the behavior of the Industrial and Rail Averages, Dow developed a theory—the famous Dow Theory—by which he sought to forecast the major direction of the stock market from the price behavior of these indices.

THEORIES AND ASSUMPTIONS

The foundations for modern technical analysis of stock trends were laid by Charles Henry Dow, a founder and the first editor of the *Wall Street Journal*. During his tenure as editor, from July 8, 1889 until his death on December 4, 1902, Dow published his observations on the market and its likely future direction based on the interactions between the Industrial and Railroad averages. These editorials constitute the solid core of present-day Dow Theory.

The Industrials represent the strongest and biggest companies called "Blue Chips" or primary issues. These companies are in goods and services. The Transports are secondary issues that move goods and people such as Rails, Trucks, Barges, and Airlines.

The two basic assumptions of Dow Theory technical analysis are:

1. That "the averages, in their day-to-day fluctuations, discount everything known, everything foreseeable, and every condition which can affect the supply of or the demand for corporate securities;" and

2. That the market moves in Trends, upward or downward, over period of time. The fundamental premise of technical analysis is that it is possible to identify and predict the Continuations and turning points in market Trends, to evaluate relative strength or weakness in the market, and to profit from the application of that analysis.

The central method of Dow Theory involves examining the co-movements of two averages, such as the Dow Jones Industrials and the Dow Jones Transportations, for "confirmations." One average is usually regarded as the primary one and the other as the confirming index. Confirmation occurs when, for instance, the Industrials reach a high above their previous high, and the Transportations do likewise around the same time. The Trend in the averages is held far more likely to continue when confirmation is present than when it is absent.

In addition, technicians have used the Dow Jones Transportation Average as a confirming indicator to the Industrials since the days of Charles H. Dow. At that time, the junior average consisted only of railroad stocks. The Industrials were considered an index of productive activity and the Rails one of distributive activity. Both of these should be sound in order to have a healthy economy, and, hence, a healthy stock market. While the Rails do not "move the nation" now as they did then, today's Transportation Index still provides a supplementary barometer of speculation in the market and, therefore, continues to be useful.

2

The technician's assumption is that if confirmation occurs between the Industrials and either of these supplementary indicators, (or more strongly, both), a Trend under way would be likely to continue. If confirmation were not present, the averages would be said to be "out of gear," and the Trend in the Industrials would be less likely to continue.

The usefulness of this, if it were true, would not be confined to the narrow Dow Jones Averages alone. Correlation among all the major averages is of a high degree and well-established historically.

The technician's assumption about confirmations and Trends appeared to us to be easy enough to test. Confirmations are visible on charts, as are subsequent movements in the averages. We, therefore, set out to test whether any statistically valid, identifiable connection exists between confirmations and subsequent Continuations of Trends.

Several of the basic principles of technical analysis extended from Dow's Theory of overall stock market behavior and applied to individual stocks, however, deserves attention.

BASIC TENETS OF TECHNICAL ANALYSIS

A. The first major principle of technical analysis is that **the market action of an individual stock reflects all the known factors affecting that stock's future.** Among the factors, and expressed in its chart, are the *general market conditions* which influence all stocks to a greater or lesser degree, as well as the particular conditions applying to the particular stock, including the trading of insiders.

A basic tenet of the Dow Theory is that *the averages discount everything (except "Acts of God")*. In technical analysis, *price and volume are the great "data reducers of the stock market"*—for individual stocks as well as for the averages. By concentrating on the interpretation of price and volume patterns only, and by disregarding the never-ending stream of corporate information, advisors' opinions, rumors, and tips and hunches from well-meaning friends, the technical analyst approaches common stock selection in a systematic manner, ideally suited for fast-moving markets were timely judgment and decisive action invariably spell the difference between success and failure.

B. The second basic principle or premise is that **stocks move in Trends.**

C. The third basic principle is that **volume goes with the Trend.** In an Uptrend, volume rises as prices rise, and declines as prices decline. Contrary behavior by a stock in an Uptrend may signal an important topping out, or reversal, in the near future.

For those of you who are thinking that this is obvious, we would point out that it is frequently not the case. Price peaks and valleys often occur during periods of low trading activity. This provides the technician with a clear signal that buying or selling pressure is abating and a new price trend is forming.

D. The fourth, and last, basic premise of technical analysis is that **a Trend, once established, tends to continue.** Until such time as its Reversal has been signalled, a Trend is assumed to continue in effect. This proposition is essentially stating an important probability—the likelihood that the next move in a stock will be in the same direction as the previous one.

STOCK IN UPTREND

An Uptrend is considered to be in force as long as each successive rally reaches a higher price than the one before it, and each successive reaction stops at a higher level than the previous reaction. A similar definition holds for a Downtrend. We divide a Trend into three subcategories:

A. The **Major Trend** usually lasts a year or more and results in appreciation or depreciation of 20% or more.

B. The **Intermediate Trend** operates in the opposite direction of the Major Trend, usually retracing one-half or less of the prior movement in the direction of the Major Trend. It is often referred to as an Intermediate Reaction.

C. **Minor Trends** consist of day-to-day fluctuations which are unimportant except as they combine to form larger Trends.

For our purposes, it will be more instructive to discuss some of the basic assumptions a technician makes in interpreting a chart. This discussion must begin with the relationship of volume and stock price. The rule of thumb is that when stock price and volume rise together, there is sufficient buying pressure to indicate an Uptrend. Conversely, although not as directly proportional, price declines will be accompanied by increasing volume if there is sufficient selling pressure to indicate a Downtrend.

Chapter 2:
Support and Resistance

STOCK "A"

CONGESTION RANGE

HOW RESISTANCE FORMS

SUPPORT ZONE (A-B)

HOW SUPPORT FORMS

STOCK "B"

RESISTANCE LEVEL

SUPPORT LEVEL

CONGESTION OR SUPPORT ZONE

OLD RESISTANCE BECOMES NEW SUPPORT

For the purposes of this discussion, we may define Support as buying—actual or potential—sufficient in volume to halt a Downtrend in prices for an appreciable period. In other words, it's where the buying is. Resistance is the antithesis of Support; it is selling, actual or potential, sufficient in volume to satisfy all bids and, hence, stop prices from going higher for a time. Support and Resistance, as they are defined, are nearly, but not quite, synonymous with supply and demand respectively.

A Support level, or zone, or band, is a price level at which sufficient demand for a stock appears to halt a Downtrend temporarily at least, and possibly reverse it, (i.e., start prices moving up again). A Resistance level, or zone, or band, by the same token, is a price level at which sufficient supply of a stock is forthcoming to stop, and possibly turn back, its Uptrend. There is, theoretically and nearly always actually, a certain amount of supply and a certain amount of demand at any given price level. (The relative amount of each will vary according to circumstances and determine the Trend.) But a Support range represents a concentration of demand, and a Resistance range represents a concentration of supply.

According to the foregoing definitions, you can see that the top boundary of a horizontal congestion pattern, such as a Rectangle, is a Resistance level, and its Bottom edge a Support level; the Top line of an Ascending Triangle is unmistakably a Resistance level.

Pullbacks and throwbacks—the quick return moves which we noted as developing so often shortly after a breakout from Head-and-Shoulders formations or other area patterns— exemplify the principles of Support and Resistance. When prices break down, for example, out of a Descending Triangle, the horizontal lower boundary of the formation which was

Analyzing Bar Charts for Profit

originally a demand line, promptly reverses its role and becomes a Resistance line. Any attempt to put prices back up through it after a decisive breakout, is stopped by supply at or near the line. By the same token, the Neckline of a Head-and-Shoulders Top, which was a demand line, becomes a Resistance level after it has been broken. The Top, or supply line of a Rectangle becomes a Support line after prices have pushed above it on volume and by a decisive margin.

VALID SUPPORT LEVELS

Major corrections or crashes, such as we had in 1929, 1962, and 1987, can change supply and demand zones fast. Panics, once they get underway, seem to sweep away all potential support in their calamitous plunges until they exhaust themselves in a general market selling climax.

Another basic premise of technical analysis is that each stock has a level of primary price Support and Resistance—in short, a price range indicating an historical balance of buying and selling pressure. In stocks with a record of volatile price activity, the range will be broader than that of a stock whose price has not fluctuated dramatically. The primary Support and Resistance levels are most obvious in stocks which have remained inactive for lengthy periods of time—technicians call this "channeling." If a stock price violates primary Support, or penetrates previous Resistance, particularly on an increase in trading volume, the technician assumes that a Trend is forming. In the case of inactive or "channeling" stocks, such a breakout often indicates dramatic future price activity.

THE "BULL" TRAP

Technical analysis also reveals the existence of second price Support levels. Stock prices do not move in a straight line. Within an Uptrend, they advance, retreat, and then advance again. Conversely, during a Downtrend, the pattern is decline, partial rebound, and further decline. Secondary price Support levels are the price ranges to which stock prices either rise or fall before resuming the dominant Trend. They are not static, but rather move with the stock price. In the case of an Uptrend, when a stock price falls below the previous secondary Support level, the technician is alerted to a potential change and, perhaps, Reversal of the dominant Trend.

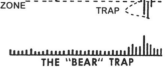

THE "BEAR" TRAP

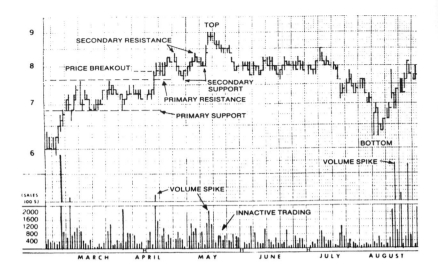

Chapter 3:
Bar Charts and Their Uses

The purpose of this discussion is to explain the nature of the bar chart, something of the history and development of the use of charts in the evaluation of securities, the philosophy and rationale of charting, some of the technical patterns seen on charts and their use and interpretation, methods and details of application and use, and comments and suggestions as to the setting up and maintaining of daily charts.

WHAT IS A BAR CHART?

A bar chart is one of the many methods of representing information in graphic form. It consists of a rectilinear grid on which two variables can be plotted. Thus, the vertical axis might be scaled to represent "miles per hour" of a moving automobile and the horizontal axis, the "rate of gasoline consumption." The vertical axis might be "total number of employees" in various industries and the horizontal axis "average wage of employees." In many kinds of engineering, sociological and economic problems, the horizontal axis represents time (hours, days, months, etc.), and the vertical axis measures the magnitude of a second variable such as population, net income, pressure, or whatever data are under examination.

In the study of securities, bar charts are widely used to show the record of price Trends and fluctuations over a period of time. These charts can be adapted to any type of financial market: stocks, bonds, warrants, debentures, commodities, etc.

They can be used for long periods, perhaps covering many years, or they may be focused down to short-term Trends on a daily or even hourly basis. [Ed. note: with today's communications, charts may be computer-generated on every tick of the market in real time.]

In charting security prices, the high and low price for the day (if it is a daily chart that is being run) are plotted on the line that represents the particular day, and the high and low are connected by a vertical line. Usually, the closing or last price for the day is shown as a cross-line on this vertical range. It is also possible to show both the opening price and the closing price, using a short line to the left of the vertical range for the opening, and a short line to the right to indicate the close. The volume of trading may be shown on a separate scale near the bottom of the sheet, directly under the vertical lines showing the daily price range. For weekly charts or monthly charts, the procedure is exactly the same except that each horizontal interval will represent a week or a month instead of a day.

It is possible to enter any other data you may be interested in directly on your chart.

Since the horizontal scale on the chart gives you a "calendar," it is possible to enter any other data you may be interested in directly on the chart. This will include, of course, ex-dividend or ex-distribution dates, the dates of stock splits, any data that might seem important as to earnings, mergers, announcements of new products, etc. By noting on the proper date the purchase or sale of a stock and the price paid or received, you will have a record of these transactions right on the chart; this will make it easy to check the status of a transaction, the profit or loss on it, and this record will serve as a valuable study later as to the degree of success of your decisions.

THE USES AND APPLICATIONS OF CHARTS

Before anyone can use any method in business, or finance, or science, or any other field, and before he can judge properly the usefulness of the method, he should have some background of theory and the goals he hopes to reach. At this point we want to consider some of this important background.

We have already spoken of the use of charts simply as a record of stock prices and trading volume—in other words, the market action of the stock—and also of the convenience of recording other data on the chart itself rather than in separate notebooks or tables.

Analyzing Bar Charts for Profit

A more important use of the chart is in back-checking the results of one's judgment, building up a body of first-hand experience in a form that can be consulted and analyzed later, and in acquiring better perception—learning from both one's past successes and failures.

To many people, the stock market is a confusing and confused mêlée in which prices move helter-skelter without rhyme or reason. But this confusion is, to some extent, a confusion in their own minds, since they do not understand the complicated forces and the detail of procedure that actually cause stock prices to advance or decline. They might feel the same sense of meaningless movement that a visitor to a textile mill might feel the first time he saw the operation of an automatic loom. He might not understand at first sight that the strange shifts of the jacquard mechanism were not meaningless, but were directed toward the orderly creation of a definite pattern in the cloth which would have meaning to anyone when he saw the finished product.

Groups of students in technical analysis of stock trends are often skeptical as to the meaning or orderliness of the market at the first or second lectures in a course. When they discover, as they do, that the long-term Trends of stocks, covering a period of a number of years, show definite Trends which often appear as straight-line channels on semi-logarithmic charting paper, they are likely to be overcome with enthusiasm, sometimes to the point where it is necessary to warn them that the existence of Trends, though true, is not the entire key to success in the stock market, but merely one of a number of important facts that appear in the study of charts. In this field, "a little" knowledge can be a very dangerous thing indeed.

The existence of trends, though true, is not the entire key to success in the stock market.

The question, at this point, is, of course, whether the charts have predictive value—whether they can be of help in planning the purchase or sale of stocks with respect to the future movement of stock prices. As to this we have a very definite opinion that they do. But if you are planning to use charts in your own financial planning, you should understand as thoroughly as possible the theory and application of them.

You should learn some of the characteristic behaviors of stock charts, check and verify what you have read and heard by your own current observations, and have some idea of what may be abstracted or surmised from a chart, and with what degree of dependability.

You have seen the gypsy shops set up in vacant stores along the second- or third-rate business streets of many of our cities. Today there is an empty store with a "For Rent" sign pasted in the window. Tomorrow the windows will be hung with printed cotton fabric; there will be displays in the window of the signs of the zodiac and various arcane symbols, and somewhere there is a display card announcing that Madame Zoloft or Princess Osira will read your character and that she sees the past, the present, and the future, clearly. If Madame Zoloft reveals the future to you, tells you that you will meet a dark woman, that you will come into a large sum of money, that you will travel across the water, this is prediction of the future. But not very good prediction.

On the other hand, every one of us makes predictions involving the future every day of our lives. In fact, we depend on our ability to predict; we could not live or work without it. Whenever a man tells his wife he will be home for dinner at 6:30, that is a prediction of the future. Whenever he writes down the date of a convention, or trip, or theater party, he makes a prediction of the future. Whenever he enters into a business transaction, gets married, buys a home, purchases stock, he makes predictions, that is to say, he considers certain known facts, weighs and evaluates them, and arrives at some conclusions as to the probable (future) consequences of his decisions.

> *Predictions can be foolish, they can be based on false data, or obsolete data; the conclusions may not follow validly from the facts at hand.*

There is nothing mystical about the predicting process; there is nothing that automatically ensures that a man's predictions (or, as we say, judgments and evaluations) are wise or valid. They can be foolish, they can be based on false data or inadequate data, or obsolete data; the conclusions may not follow validly from the facts at hand.

But, the degree of a man's success will depend on his ability to abstract the relevant facts, to weigh them and determine their importance, and to arrive at the best decisions possible from the data available. The results of his past experiments and experience, if he relates these to future problems as they arise, constitute the background of understanding which we call "intuition." If he is observant and uses each new experience to correct and add to the body of knowledge he has already, he will have, in effect, a cybernetic machine, a perceptual ability to continue learning and to correct his own methods, to improve accuracy, to update the basis of his premises, and to modify his predictions in line with changing conditions.

All this can be said in a single paragraph. But sound judgment, good intuition, foresight and wisdom do not come about overnight by reading a book or adopting a method or discovering a formula. These invaluable assets on which our vital predictive processes in life are based constitute a whole lifelong process of self-education. It is not easy, but it is the only way.

THE LIMITATIONS OF PREDICTIVE METHODS

Good predictive ability is not only difficult—it is also not "absolute." When we choose a wife, or build a business, or buy a stock, we are making the best decisions we know how to with the best current evidence we can get. All we can hope for is to make the best choice of several in the light of the present situation. All we have to go on is what we have learned in the past. Our experiences with women will aid us in choosing the right wife. What we have learned about business will help in choosing the right products, the right location, the right kind of organization. And what we have learned from past experience about stocks will be our best guide as to buying the right stocks now. This is what is meant by good prediction.

If the conditions change, if new facts appear, it will be necessary to overhaul the prediction and alter it accordingly; or, in some cases, to reject it entirely and make a fresh start.

There is nothing in any prediction of the future that is absolute or that guarantees the outcome. But there is a vast difference in the degree of probability between Madame Zoloft's prediction of coming into a large sum of money and the weather bureau's prediction of a cold front moving into the New England area within the next twenty-four hours. The last prediction has a high degree of probability. When the astronomers tell us that there will be a total eclipse of the sun on March 18, 1988, with totality lasting three minutes, and visibility in Sumatra, this is a prediction with a very high degree of probability.

In ordinary human affairs we do not need and cannot expect certainty in our judgments and evaluations. This is because the uncertainty principle is as much a part of living as life itself (which is also uncertain). Yet, with anything as uncertain as the duration of human life, the insurance companies make their actuarial tables on the basis of their past experience; and because of the vast experience they have to draw on, these are, over the long pull, exceedingly accurate.

Humility is the first and foremost need of a stock analyst.

If we say, as we have said, and say once again here, that humility is the first and foremost need of a stock analyst, investor, or trader, this is not the kind of humility that hangs its head in shameful ignorance. Because a man admits he "does not know everything," it is not necessary for him also to confess that he "does not know anything." There are all shades of knowledge and experience, or the lack of them, between total ignorance and omniscience. If there is one factor that stands in the way of a reasonable and practical use of stock charts or any other market tool, it is the feeling that one must be completely right or one is completely wrong.

But, if a particular method, or study, or point of view can do nothing more than improve one's total performance a bit on balance, then it is worthwhile. In fact, if it can aid a man in eliminating some of his worst habitual mistakes, it can be very valuable indeed. It can improve his "batting average" greatly.

As a prelude to any technical study of the market, it would be well for the serious student to do some reading in psychology, perception, general semantics, etc., in order to understand the workings of his own mind, so that he can see clearly what he is trying to do and how he can apply new knowledge and experience. This type of study should come first since most of the real tragedies of investment come about through: (a) inadequate or obsolete information; (b) mis-evaluation of the information; (c) faulty conclusions from the data; and, perhaps most importantly, (d) stubborn habits of be-havior that, like rigid prejudices, are often based on poorly conceived emotions and which often fly directly in the face of verifiable facts.

Also, in connection with prediction (or call it planning, judgment, foresight, etc.), it is a good idea to have some under-standing of what kind of information and what kind of premise one will use as a basis. Without any orderly, consistent program, it will not be possible to check back and see what the results of past actions have been in relation to the reasons on which we based our decisions.

One could say that the technical methods, like any method of prediction, involves looking at the past, checking whether the present conditions are greatly different and, if so, making allowances for the differences, and then making cer-tain conclusions, based on these studies, as to what seems most likely to happen in the future.

This is not a particularly mysterious process. Although, in its details, it may involve a tremendous amount of sheer labor. The principles involved are simple enough.

For example, if I have the past record of a series of num-bers and the series runs as follows: 7, 7, 7, 7, 7, 7, 7, 7, and the present term of the series is 7, I would predict, with some con-fidence, that the next (future) term will be 7.

If the past series runs: 3, 4, 5, 6, 7, 8, 9, 10, and the present term of the series is 11, I would predict that the next term will be 12.

If the past series runs: 3, 6, 11, 4, 48, 96, and the present term is 19, I would predict that the next term will be 384.

Depending on the total picture one has, one may look for a continuation of a constant number, or an arithmetic progression, a geometric progression, an exponential progression, a cyclic or wave-like rhythm, or any form that seems to fit the past and present facts, projected in the future, as if we were continuing some sort of "orderly" pattern.

The trick, of course, is to find the "orderly" pattern, which may not be a simple function, but may be a combination of several quite different functions.

Also, one must be careful not to let one's enthusiasm run wild to a point where one "sees" patterns and rhythms where none actually exist.

And, of course, it is necessary to be on guard all the time against the various "pitfalls" we have discussed, the prejudices and attitudes that are so ingrained in us that they may distort our vision and "slant" our evaluation.

It is because these "ingrained" opinions are so deeply a part of our value systems that they can be so damaging if they are distorting our perception of the facts. That may be why it is almost impossible to "learn" stock trading or commodity trading solely from reading a book or attending a class. It requires days, weeks, months, sometimes years, of personal close observation and experience to implement the reading or the classroom study. It takes that time and that experience to revise the old and sometimes faulty concepts. For they are not going to erase themselves or amend themselves just on the strength of your intellectual acceptance of a new viewpoint alone. The new ideas must be developed until they become the "habitual" responses.

One of the "old" tendencies that can be a dangerous pitfall is to predict in terms of a change in the Major Trend. This probably comes out of a whole complicated evaluation in which we appraise a stock according to certain "fundamental" facts about the company it represents. Such an attitude can lead to a frame of mind where any considerable advance in the price of a stock leads to a certain habitual response; namely that the stock is "over-valued" in the market. The conclusion, of course, is that eventually the stock will "find its *true* value"; and the prediction from all of this will be that the stock should be sold.

The same situation in reverse occurs when a stock has declined sharply. The tendency is to feel that the stock "is priced too low," is "under-valued," "can't go much lower," etc. And, these reactions lead to a prediction that the stock will shortly advance in price, and, therefore, that it should be bought.

Sometimes this type of prediction (that the Trend will reverse itself) will be confirmed in the future action of the stock. However, before pinning too much confidence in this particular method, it would be well advised to check the record of past predictions made on this basis. You may find that it is much harder than you thought to predict, even approximately, when or where the turning point will come.

For myself, I would prefer to make exactly the opposite prediction. If I had only the choice of predicting a *Reversal* of the Major Trend, or a *Continuation* of the Major Trend, I would have to choose the Continuation. As Robert D. Edwards has put it, I would agree that "A Trend should be assumed to continue in effect until such time as its Reversal has been definitely signaled."

However, what we are talking about here is not the detail of prediction, not the application of technical methods, it is something much more basic; the limits of prediction. If you consider the question of whether the Trend or direction of a stock's price should be predicted in the expectation of a Reversal of the Major Trend, or in the expectation of a Continuation, you will see that we are once again talking about an "either/or" situation. And, wherever we can, we try to frame the problem so that we can change the "either/or" into a matter of *degree*. Then we will be able to answer the question in several or many ways, and not in just two ways.

> *"A Trend should be assumed to continue in effect until such time as its Reversal has been definitely signaled."*
>
> —*Robert D. Edwards*

Sometimes, as in this case, we cannot exactly change the "either/or" question to one of degree; but, we can do something that serves much the same purpose. We can reduce it to a "probability."

If you say BankAmerica is "going to go up," and I say BankAmerica is "going to go down," then in a month or after whatever time we agree on, you can take a look at it, and say, "You were right," or "I was right." If the stock has gone up, you would be *right*, in this situation. And, if it has gone down, then I would be *right*.

And this, again, is the two-valued situation, the "either/or." Which is what we are trying to avoid.

You see, in this view, if your predictive method is "right" it will give you the "right" result. If the stock goes up in price, then you are "right," and your prediction is "right," and your predictive method is "right." But if the stock goes down, then you are "wrong," your prediction is "wrong," and your predictive method is "wrong."

This leads to trouble. You might be quite "right" about BankAmerica this month. You might be "right" about Advanced Micro Devices next month, and about B.F. Goodrich the following month. But, sooner or later, you will be "wrong" on one. This, almost by definition, makes your method itself "wrong," at least in that particular case. It either discredits your method entirely, or it casts a shadow and a doubt on it. At the very least, it destroys your confidence.

Let me suggest here that you consider for a moment *other* kinds of prediction, outside of the market. You will see how this same failure and demoralization can occur wherever you attempt to set up a "perfect" "either/or" predictive method.

But we don't have to do it in a two-valued, absolute way! We can recognize certain limits of predictive expectation in terms of probabilities; and then we will not continually be afraid to use our method because of our lack of confidence in it. We will not be expecting more from our method than we can reasonably hope for. And we will not be basing our method on a few accidental "successes."

Is this clear? Do you see that a very stupid method of prediction (such as betting even money that one can draw a spade from an ordinary deck of cards) could at times produce a succession of "wins." If you should see someone make such a bet over and over again, would you feel it was a "right" method of prediction; even if he won eight times in succession?

Or, to put it another way, suppose you were to have the chance of betting even money you would *not* draw a spade from the deck. Every time you drew a heart or a diamond, or a club you would win. Only when you drew a spade would you lose.

Under these conditions, if you were to lose several times in a row on this bet, would you discard your method as "wrong?" Would you reverse your method and bet that you would draw a spade, merely because of a run of luck against you?

Isn't it possible to say that, providing the deck of cards is an honest one, containing the usual cards and properly shuffled, it makes *no difference* how many times you "win" or how many times you "lose"? This does not affect the "rightness" or "wrongness" of your method of evaluation. And your best policy is to continue to use your evaluative method as long as you are convinced that it is based on adequate data and valid reasoning.

Of course, you know this. You know this from what you have previously abstracted from your experience in drawing cards from decks. It seems terribly redundant to have to go through this long discussion of something (perhaps an elephant stuck in your front entry) so obvious, so plain. You know that neither the roulette croupier nor the owners of the casino care very much whether you or any other player wins or loses. If the casino's bank is well-heeled, the "method of evaluation" will wear down the string of luck or the "system" of any roulette player, as every professional gambler knows.

And the method of evaluation used by the professional gambler is not based on being "absolutely right" on any particular play or series of plays, but on a prediction as to the "most probable outcome of a long series of plays taken as a whole."

Then, why is it that so many people either have no real evaluative method at all, or follow one which represents so little first-hand checking and verifying that it may be worse than useless? Could it be that because they are so deeply trained in "either/or" and "right and wrong" they cannot habituate themselves to a method based on *uncertainty*?

If we know that on the basis of past experience and in view of the present outlook we may expect to "win seven times out of ten, in an even-money series of bets," we can accept this seven-out-of-ten probability as something akin to what would be a "measure" or "degree" in some other types of problem. With certain reservations and precautions we can accept this as the measure of our expectation; and by continually re-checking and verifying we can adjust and refine this until it becomes a highly dependable tool so long as the basic conditions of the contest do not change materially.

We can operate on this basis with considerable confidence. And, with this foundation for our confidence, we will not "need to be right" all the time.

Think what this means. Consider the nights you have lain awake and worried about what "the market" would do tomorrow, or whether "XYZ" would go up or down before the end of the week. You will not be able to eliminate *all* anxiety about the market, but you will be able to greatly reduce the amount of your tension and worry since you will not feel threatened with a "total failure" of your method every time a stock moves a point or so "against" you.

What we have done here is to set some limits on the predictive science. The average person seems to recognize no limits whatever. What they so often seek and insist upon is an infallible method of reading the future. And they are so sure that if they only keep trying and searching they will come up with the "right" method, that charlatans mulct him of millions of dollars every year by supplying spurious "perfect systems." (And this is also true on many other streets besides Wall Street.)

We have set limits. We have stopped short of the "100%" upper limit, representing infallibility, and we have set our goal considerably above the "0" of the thoroughly discouraged cynic who feels it is "all just luck."

By observing the results of a method as applied in the past, and noting the number of successes and failures, we can gauge the (past) success of the method. We can then project these results into the future as a probability, and say, "I believe, on the basis of the past records, this method will probably produce an average net return of between 20% and 30% per year."

That statement isn't nearly positive enough to satisfy the individual trained to think in absolute terms. Neither is the expected return anywhere near as large as such a person would expect (on the basis that he will "always be right"). Neither is it definite enough; for that person we are speaking of does not think in terms of "somewhere between." They want it right out plain and sharp.

Of course, the chances of our being "totally defeated" are much less than theirs. But, for them, it is necessary to "reach the Top" and that means shooting at nothing short of perfection.

The novice in the market, as in other fields, is likely to shy away from anything "technical" and which he does not understand. He is likely to prefer what he will consider a "common-sense" approach, usually based on cause-and-effect reasoning. In other words, this will probably happen because of that. The price of the stock will advance because of a coming merger and announced improvement in earnings, etc. This may be true at times. Although, the novice will also attach a great deal more certainty to his conclusions than a more experienced man and

The novice will tend to concentrate on a single fact or reason as the cause, overlooking the multitude of other conditions that can affect the outcome greatly.

will tend to concentrate on a single fact or reason as the cause, overlooking the multitude of other conditions that can affect the outcome greatly. At best, he will probably consider only a few selected data and will not take into account the remaining factors, or he will attribute far more weight to his reasons than experience in these matters would substantiate.

Add to this the difficulty of evaluating the various products of a company, particularly when so many corporations today are widely diversified and may include many divisions engaged in entirely different fields. Sometimes the key to a situation may lie in the development of some new process or product by a hitherto obscure subsidiary. Often, it is possible to give several or many reasons why a stock should be behaving in a certain way. And, it is possible that the most important reason behind a Trend might be entirely overlooked. And, in some cases, the real reasons might not be known or available to the public at all. This last could be the case where steps were being taken by some outside group to acquire control of a company where a campaign for a change of management was building up.

On top of all these reasons why stock prices may move, there are also many others which are not directly connected with the business of the company represented by the stock at all—monetary changes, inflation and deflation, the general prosperity or depression of the country's economy, various political factors, and also the prevailing "psychological mood" of investors. There are times when investors generally are optimistic, when there is a feeling of confidence; and there are times when the investing public feels discouraged, is not interested very much in stocks at any price, and when the market reflects only the general apathy.

Obviously, it is not possible to evaluate all of these factors —many of them debatable, some unverifiable, and others intangible—by the same kind of methods one would use to analyze a chemical, balance a set of books, or measure a tract of land. The problem is not only vastly more complicated; it also means reducing to a common denominator matters of fact, matters of judgment, and matters of speculation as to the probable future course of things. On the basis of statistics, news, factual information, etc., it would not be possible for six men working independently to arrive at identical "values" for the stock of a company. Not unless, by common agreement, they all used a common formula agreed upon in advance, omitting many of the debatable and unverifiable points; and then, of course, the values determined would not be independent and, in any case, would represent only the arbitrary valuations according to the rule or formula.

It is important to understand this. Otherwise, the daily chart means nothing, and, for that matter, the market itself means nothing. For if there were any complete and precise formula for determining the value of a stock in dollars and cents, then the democratic auction of the market itself would be meaningless whenever the market price did not coincide with the formula price.

But, from the very practical angle of what we can get for a stock if we want to sell it, or what we will have to pay for it if we want to buy it, the market price is the valuation we have to accept. If a stock is selling at $50 a share and you and I and others feel it is worth less, or if we feel it probably will be worth less, or if we need to raise some money by selling stock, then, if enough people are selling enough stock, this supply will tend to bring the price down to $49, to $48, or lower, depending on the amount of stock offered and the urgency of the selling. On the other hand, if we should feel that this same stock is worth more than $50, or that it probably will be worth more; then we would be buying it, and our bids would use up the supply of stock offered at $50 and we might have to pay $51, $52 or more.

Anyone has the right to feel that $50 is too high or too low a price for a stock. If he feels that $50 is too high a price to pay, he can bid $40 for it, but he will not get it as long as there are others willing to pay more. Or if he wants to sell, but feels the price of $50 is too low, he can offer his stock at $60. But, here again, he will not get his price as long as there are others willing to sell for $50.

If there were any complete precise formula for determining the value of a stock in dollars and cents, then the democratic auction of the market itself would be meaningless whenever the market price did not coincide with the formula price.

So, regardless of formulas and theories, ratios and economic breakdowns, the value of a stock, in terms of what you pay or what you get, is determined by what the investing public feels it should be. The price is the result of the bids and offers of all the investors, those who feel it should be higher, and those who feel it should be lower.

It is very easy to say, and many have said, that a price determined in this way by public auction may be unrealistic, that it might be the result of psychological forces—a wave of optimism, a spell of panic. It is true that if one had perfect insight and a complete understanding of a situation, he might set the value higher or lower than the market sets it. If he were right, and if things worked out as he anticipated, this would be highly profitable to him.

However, to set one's own opinion squarely against the judgment of the market calls for a degree of wisdom (or a degree of sheer folly) that few of us would claim. So far as the internal and corporate affairs of a company are concerned, there are officers and directors whose livelihood and business future depend on knowing their own company and its prospects. There are also employees, many of whom may also be investors in the company's stock, who are in a position, at least, to know more about what is going on than the outside stock trader. There are professional analysts and managers for large institutions—the banks, insurance companies, mutual funds, pension funds, etc. There are individual investors who may have been studying a certain industry or a certain stock for many years. When a man tells you that a particular stock, selling now, let us say, at $50, is really worth $100, you should realize that he is expressing an opinion, his own judgment, and he is setting that judgment against the serious evaluation of other investors whose dollars are at stake in this evaluation.

If we seem to have wandered a considerable distance from discussion of the charts themselves, it is because this discussion is of paramount importance in understanding what it is that charts tell us, and why we do not insist that they not only tell us what is happening, but also *why* it is happening.

To round out this section, there is one more important point that must be covered. Obviously, whatever happens in the market to a stock reflects something that somebody thinks, feels, or believes will affect the future value of that stock. The record of past earnings or dividends on the assumption of a Continuation of past performance, or the projection of a past Trend. Today's price for any stock reflects and includes all the hopes or fears anyone may have for its future. It is each man's opinion merged with the opinion of every other investor interested in the stock; and the resulting figure is the ultimate meeting point—"the bloodless verdict of the marketplace."

So, the market price at any time (which is what the chart gives us graphically) is a prediction of the future as seen through many eyes. It is the best educated guess of all those concerned.

But it should be clearly understood that while all of us have to make predictions as to the probable consequences and outcome of our action when we buy a house, when we get married, when we take a new job, or whatever we do, it is not possible to make these predictions "absolute." It might be your prediction that at five o'clock you would get your car at the parking lot and drive home in time for dinner. This might be a good and reasonable prediction of that future event. But it is possible for the conditions to change. The car might have a bad battery and might not start. There might be a highway tie-up that would prevent your getting home until very late. Your wife might have sprained her ankle and gone to bed. We have to make predictions, the best we know how. But, we must be prepared, always, to change our plans and to make a new evaluation if the situation changes in some unexpected way.

This is a key point in the use of charts or in any investment planning. It is necessary to use the best current data we can get and to apply it in the light of our experience to estimate the probable developments. But we must never become so "frozen" to today's opinion that we are unable to change it tomorrow if there is new evidence calling for "a revised map."

In discussion of the use of daily charts, we are assuming that the market price at any moment represents a meeting of bids and offers of those who want to buy and those who want to sell—therefore, the market value at that moment—and the chart provides a visual history of the market action in such a form that it is easy to see, at a glance, the Trend of the stock's price and any important changes in price Trend or in volume of trading. For such a chart, it is possible to draw some inferences and form some valid opinions as to the probable future market action. In other words, the chart is a tool; it is, in fact, merely a factual record; and its interpretation and use depends on the experience and judgment of the investor who is using it. Trends and patterns do not cause movements in the market. (We would question even the limited psychological effect they might have in influencing the Trends of large and important stocks, since large and institutional holders of stocks cannot buy or liquidate heavily overnight, and amongst individual investors only a small percentage are willing or able to act on technical market action.)

CONSTRUCTION OF A DAILY CHART

A stock chart (daily, weekly, or monthly) will ordinarily have a time scale running from left to right, covering the period included in the chart, and a vertical scale representing the price of the stock.

The horizontal time scale will be of uniform intervals. But the vertical price scale may be on any of several scales. The chart can be made on ordinary cross-section paper, or on a chart sheet having arithmetic vertical divisions. In this case, the spacing is uniform from bottom to top, and the distance between 10 and 20 will be the same as the distance between 20 and 30, or between 80 and 90.

Or, the vertical scale may be on logarithmic, square root, cube root, or some other scale. In such cases, the scale will usually give a larger vertical distance to a lower-priced stock, and, as the price advances, the vertical scale becomes more compressed. Thus, the distance between 10 and 20 will be more than the distance between 20 and 30, and again, this will be more than the distance between 80 and 90. The reason for using a scale which "shrinks" as the price advances is that, obviously, an advance of 5 points in a stock selling at $10 is much more important in its effect on capital than an advance of 5 points in a stock selling at $50. In the first case, the 5 points would represent a gain of 50%, in the second case, only 10%.

Since what we are concerned with is the percentage change in capital represented by a price move, there is a great deal to be said for using what is known as a percentage, ratio, or logarithmic scale. The characteristic of this scale is that it will measure percentage advances or declines directly, and a move of 10% or 35%, or any other percentage, will always appear as the same vertical distance on the chart regardless of the price of the stock. Thus, chartwise, a move from $1,000 a share to $1,500 a share would look exactly like an advance from $10 to $15, or from $50 to $75; any advance of 50% in a stock would cover the same vertical distance. This makes it possible to compare the action of a stock with any other stock directly, or to compare the action of a stock with a group average, or to compare stocks or groups with general market averages similarly scaled.

The objection one sometimes hears about logarithmic charts is that the "squeezing" of the scale as the price advances makes it impossible to chart precisely to the last eighth when the price has moved up greatly. In other words, a move of 1/8 point will be shown plainly on stocks in the 10s and 20s but will not show precisely on stocks selling in the 100s. But, one should realize a move of 1/8 point is quite important, say when a stock is selling at $5 a share, and is insignificant on one that is quoted at $150.

The other question new users bring up regarding the logarithmic scale is that continually "shrinking" intervals seems strange (at first) to them if they have been used to using plain cross-section paper, that is, arithmetically scaled sheets. Actually, the changing log scale provides points of reference which the eye soon learns to recognize, and there is less chance

What we are concerned with is the percentage change in capital represented by a price move, there is a great deal to be said for using what is known as a percentage, ratio, or logarithmic scale.

A move of 1/8 point is quite important, say, when a stock is selling at $5 a share, and is insignificant on one that is quoted at $150.

of entering a price at the wrong place than when using paper that has a perfectly uniform scale.

HOW TO USE TEKNIPLAT CHART PAPER

If you have never kept charts on this type of paper, known as semi-logarithmic, ratio, or proportion, these instructions will help you to read and understand the charts more easily, and they will help you in getting started if you are setting up charts of your own.

There will be no problem here for the engineer or the experienced chartist, but many people who have not kept charts before, or who are familiar only with the arithmetic price scale where the intervals are uniform throughout, may be puzzled at first by the continually changing vertical spaces. As you will discover, however, this very feature makes for easier and faster charting, because the various prices always lie at the same point in one of the "banks," and the eye becomes adept in placing the point needed automatically, without reference to the index figures along the left margin.

On many simple charts, showing hours of work, temperature changes, depth of water, etc., it is perfectly satisfactory to use ordinary cross-section paper, so that each hour, degree, or foot is represented by the same vertical distance on the chart. The difference between 5 feet and 10 feet is the same as the distance between 105 feet and 110 feet.

But this is not a good way to represent the differences in stock prices. It is perfectly true that the difference in market value between a stock selling at $5 a share and one selling at $10 a share is $5, or $500 on a block of 100 shares. And that the difference between the value of a stock selling at $100 and one at $105 is also $5, or $500 on a block of 100 shares. But, in this latter case, there is a great deal more of your capital involved.

For example, if you put $1,000 into a stock at $5 you would get (disregarding commission) 200 shares. And if you sold these at $10 you will receive $2,000. You would have a profit of $1,000, or 100%. But, if you put your $1,000 into a stock selling at $105, you would be able to buy only 9 shares. And when you sold five points higher at $110, your profit would be only $45 or 4 1/2%.

It will give you a better comparison of the percentages of profit in various stock transactions if the price scale of your chart is designed to show equal percentages of advance or decline as equal vertical distances, regardless of the price of the stock. This is exactly what the TEKNIPLAT charting paper does. A certain vertical distance on the paper will always indicate the same percentage change, and a Trend moving at a certain angle will always indicate the same rate of percentage change, no matter what the price of the stock may be.

Obviously, one point of advance or decline is much more important to you in a stock selling at $5 or $6 a share than in one selling at $100. So it should not surprise you that the interval between $5 and $6 is much larger than that between $100 and $101. And, since the stocks at lower prices make larger percentage moves for each point, or half point, or one-eighth point, these moves will show up more plainly on their charts. Actually, it is not possible on the TEKNIPLAT paper to show a single eighth of change for a stock selling as high as $100. But this is just another way of saying that a single eighth is not important at that price. You might well be concerned about the difference between 1 1/4 and 1 3/8. But you would not care too much whether you sold at 103 or 103 1/8.

Since all your stocks will be plotted on a proportional basis, you can compare directly the action of any one stock with any other as to pattern, Trend, etc. Thus, a stock selling at $16 can be compared with a stock selling at $56. However, although the percentages moves will be strictly comparable, it should be pointed out that typically, the very high-priced issues make smaller percentage moves than the low-priced ones.

COPYRIGHT 1961 BY JOHN MAGEE, SPRINGFIELD, MASS.

Type RU

Published and Distributed by **JOHN MAGEE, Inc.**   Technical Analysis of Stock Trends, 65 Broad Street, Boston, MA 02109

(SALES 100'S)

Analyzing Bar Charts for Profit

THE PRICE SCALE

The price scale on TEKNIPLAT paper consists of two "banks," occupying the upper and lower halves of the main chart space. These two banks are exactly alike. Each represents a doubling of prices from its bottom to its top, so that whatever value is assigned to the center line, the top line will be twice that figure and the bottom line will be half of it. Let us say the center point is marked 20; then the top will be 40 and the nine intermediate lines will be 22, 24, 26, 28, 30, 32, 34, 36 and 38, reading from center to top, with each of the smallest spaces representing 1/4 point. In the lower half of the chart, the bottom line will be 10, the intermediate heavy lines to the center will be 11, 12, 13, 14, 15, 16, 17, 18 and 19, and each of the smallest spaces will be 1/8 point. Since the spaces get smaller as one goes up the chart, one bank shades into the next, making a continuous scale. Obviously, you could have 20 at the top, 10 at the center and 5 at the bottom; or 10 at the top, 5 at the center and 2 1/2 at the bottom.

You may have some trouble at first with the different values assigned to the small spaces at different price levels; you may wonder whether a single small space represents 1/4 or 1/8 or perhaps a full point. Do not let this bother you. You can see from the scale where 19 is and where 20 is, and obviously 19 1/2 is the mid-point, 19 1/4 is one-quarter of the way up, and so on. Very quickly, you will find that your mind and your eye adjust almost instantly without any conscious thought or effort.

Where a stock goes off the top or bottom of the paper, it is a simple matter to re-scale by moving the chart scale down one bank. If the chart runs off the top at 40, mark the center of the paper 40 and then on—the top becomes 80 and the bottom, 20.

For uniformity, and because the paper is so ruled that you can divide either bank of the heavy intermediate lines into ten parts, with smaller spaces representing standard stock-trading fractions of these main divisions, you must use the figures 5, 10, 20, 40, 80, etc., as the values for the center lines, tops and bottoms of charts.

For selection of scales on stocks for which you are starting new charts, use the table below.

If the Stock Now Sells Between	Will Be	Center Line Top	Bottom
224 and 448	320	640	160
112 and 224	160	320	80
56 and 112	80	160	40
28 and 56	40	80	20
14 and 28	20	40	10
7 and 14	10	20	5
3 1/2 and 7	5	10	2 1/2
1 3/4 and 3 1/2	2 1/2	5	1 1/4

(This table can, of course, be continued up or down as far as necessary by multiplying or dividing the key figures by two.)

THE TIME SCALE

The paper provides for a full year of charting. The sheet is divided into 53 weeks, each consisting of six days in which the heavier line represents a Saturday, and this is ordinarily left blank since the major markets are not open on Saturday. However, the heavier line will serve to make it easier to locate a day within a week, quickly. The omission of the Saturday will not perceptibly affect the Trend of the technical patterns.

Holidays, when they occur, are skipped. Usually a small "H" is inserted at the bottom of the chart to note the holiday and explain the break in the chart.

Many technicians start their charts as of the first of a calendar year, filling in the dates of Saturdays marking the end of each week at the bottom of the paper in the spaces provided, and immediately above these dates, the months.

There is no reason, however, that charts cannot be started at any time, and if you keep a large number of charts, it may be a help to start some of these in each calendar quarter. Thus, you might start all charts from A to F in January, from G to M in April, from N to S in July, and from T to Z in October.

THE VOLUME SCALE

The volume scale that has proved most satisfactory is arithmetic, that is, each unit measured vertically represents the same number of shares traded.

Space for volume entries is provided in a special section above the dates. At one time, a logarithmic volume scale was used, but it was given up because the highly significant volumes on very active days tended to be compressed, while low volume in periods of dullness was given too much emphasis.

It is necessary to determine the proper figures for the volume scale. No rule for this can be suggested. It is simply a matter of trial and error. With a little experience you will be able to estimate, from your knowledge of the stock you are about to chart, about how much volume is like to appear on very active days; and you can set up a volume scale that will allow for the maximum expected peak. What you want to avoid is the situation where volume too frequently runs beyond the top of the volume section; it should do this only at times of unusual activity.

Where a stock is new to you and you have no knowledge of its habits, it may be best to mark a tentative volume scale, lightly and in pencil, and keep the volume on this scale for a few weeks. Then, if it is necessary to change the scale, you can do so without having to draw the entire chart over.

EX-DIVIDENDS AND SPLIT-UPS

When a stock goes "ex-dividend," "ex-rights," etc., the price will usually drop approximately the amount of the benefit that was "ex." A note should be made on the chart on this day and this can be entered conveniently at the very bottom, below the dates, showing the amount of the dividend, approximate value of the rights, or other benefits. If the amount involved was substantial and the price drop is large enough to require explanation, a dotted line may be drawn vertically on that date from the old price to the "ex" price, showing that this drop was not a market fluctuation, but merely the adjustment of price to the distribution.

In the case of a split-up, spin-off, or other capital change, a similar procedure is followed. If the stock is split three-shares-for-one, for example, the price level will change and the chart will be continued at a new level. A dotted vertical line plus an explanatory note will make clear what happened. In order to get continuity of the chart in such a case, the previous price pattern can be traced and then transferred with carbon paper in the correct position to give a continuous chart adjusted to the new basis for as far back as you need it.

However, if a stock is split two-shares-for-one or four-for-one, you will not have to make any change in the chart except to note the fact of the split, and to change the scale by dividing all figures by 2 or 4 as the case may be.

In other words, if a stock has been selling at $80 and is split two-for-one, we simply re-scale the chart with the price at $40 and carry on. Very often it will help to rule a vertical red line through the date on which a split-up or other capital adjustment takes effect.

Just to reiterate what has been explained above regarding the mechanical details of charting:

1. Ordinarily, each day's high and low prices are connected by a vertical line, and the last or closing price is indicated by a short horizontal line which may be

drawn toward the right, and open, if used is drawn to the left. Volume is shown on a special scale at the bottom of the chart, and notes as to ex-dividend dates and amounts of dividends, ex-rights, ex-distributions, split-ups, stock dividends, etc. may be noted as they occur below the volume. Other notes, clippings, record of purchase and sale, and other memos may be written or attached to the chart where they will be conveniently at hand each day.

2. The TEKNIPLAT charting paper is ruled for a six-day week, although the market operates only from Monday through Friday. The heavy line indicating a Saturday is not used, but, because it provides a little break each week, it makes the plotting of the market days much easier, and this does not materially affect the accuracy of the chart, nor does it distort appreciably the Trendlines, patterns, etc. Holidays that occur during the business week are simply skipped and left blank, and the fact that the omitted day was a holiday may be indicated by placing the letter "H" at the bottom of the chart.

The most important factor in charting, of course, is to keep the charts up to date. It will pay to take some time to plan how, and where, and when to keep one's charts. If possible, find a place, at home or at your office, where you can be relatively free from interference for at least long enough each day to post your charts. Experiment a bit with the placement of desk or table so that you will be getting the best light possible without sharp shadows and without glare. Have binders or folders so that you can keep your charts in a convenient arrangement, easily accessible. Try out various grades of pens or pencils to find which will give you the best results. And have a definite place, a drawer or box, where you can keep an adequate supply of pencils, erasers, triangles, ruler, or whatever other equipment you may need.

The most important factor in charting, of course, is to keep the charts up to date.

One most important caution for the beginner who is starting a set of charts for the first time—do not bite off more than you can handle easily! It is a great temptation to set up a large portfolio at the very start. But when some unexpected interruption occurs, such as a day of illness, a trip out of town, or some emergency work, the charts may be neglected for a day, two days, three days, and with each passing day, the load multiplies. Many enthusiastic beginners have thus become discouraged and have given up the work before they were fairly into it. It is better to take a smaller group than you feel you might want, but which you are sure you can keep up without strain, and then with increasing speed and greater familiarity with the method, to add stocks gradually as needed.

THE BLOODLESS VERDICT OF THE MARKETPLACE

If you have followed the line of reasoning in the preceding sections, especially that part which touches on the difficulty of knowing all about a corporation or about the market as a whole, you will realize that the most dependable criterion of value in the practical sense of what you must pay, or what you can get for something (whether it should be shares of stock, bushels of wheat, land, houses, automobiles, or whatever), is the free speculative auction in which the bids and offers of prospective buyers and sellers determine the price. Whether the reasons behind these bids and offers are sound, or reasonable, or wise, has nothing to do with the fact that the price is determined by them and any investor is at liberty to take it or leave it.

There is an implication here that men who are putting their own hard-earned cash on the line to support their opinions are likely to have serious reasons for doing so; there is at least a presumption that the composite of these opinions, the consensus as represented by the price at a given moment, may be the most realistic expression of value we can hope to get.

Therefore, following this line of reasoning, we must assume that the current price of the stock represents all that is known, or believed, or hoped, or feared, in connection with the present value of future probable value of that stock.

Analyzing Bar Charts for Profit

THE CHARTS SIMPLY REFLECT HUMAN EVALUATION

The question is sometimes raised as to whether a stock chart will reflect unreasoning emotional states of mind on the part of investors. That is surely true at times. There have been "crazy" booms in stocks; and there have been equally "crazy" collapses and panics. But, the fact that these market actions cannot always be supported by factual reports and statistics does not make them any less important. When the price of a stock starts to climb or when the bottom falls out of it, it is best to take appropriate action, recognizing that an important move is taking place, rather than trying to hold back the tide because it doesn't seem to make any sense. In a surprising number of cases, the move eventually does prove to make sense, the collective judgment of the market is extremely sensitive and perceptive as to probable changes in production, earnings, dividends, and other matters affecting the affairs of a company.

If a market move turns out to be premature or false, if the expected, or hoped for, or feared, developments do not come about, it is still true that one cannot argue with the tape. It is best, we feel, to accept the facts regardless of the reasons, assuming that in most cases the reasoning behind the move is sound.

There remains one other question which we feel has always been given more weight than it deserves, especially by those who have not studied too long or too deeply. The question is whether the movement may represent merely the manipulative operations of dishonest traders, or whether, through false rumors, or merely through the fact that something seems to be happening, the movement snowballs and accelerates on its own momentum.

So far as dishonest manipulation is concerned, this has never been an entirely safe or easy thing, even in the "bad old days" when no punches were barred. Today, with the various regulatory laws and the rules of procedure in the important Exchanges, plus the self-protective, self-regulation of the

When the price of a stock starts to climb or when the bottom falls out of it, it is best to take appropriate action, recognizing that an important move is taking place, rather than trying to hold back the tide because it doesn't seem to make any sense.

reputable brokerage houses, it is more difficult. Still, as the various insider trading trials prove, there will always be a dishonest element in the market.

Nor do we believe that the important market moves are merely the result of rumor, collective hysteria, and emotional confusion. There are too many hardheaded men, both individuals and traders for institutions, who are prepared to check and counterbalance an entirely capricious or irrational move. We would question whether the recommendations of brokers or investment advisory services, or the statements of newspaper writers or radio and TV analysts, or the self-reflexive action of technical factors are major elements in important market moves.

In all of this, in all of the changes shown in the charts (which are a picture of what is actually happening in the market and which is indirectly a portrayal of what the collective investing public is perceiving), we are dealing with speculation. In this connection, we are using the word in the particular sense in which *Webster's Ninth New International Dictionary* defines it, in the first definition of the word as in current use: "The faculty, act, or process of intellectual examination or investigation." This is the proper and legitimate function of a market and in no way implies any dishonorable or unfair practice. The word, as Webster here defines it, is merely synonymous with evaluation, and it is in this sense that we use it in this treatise.

THE TECHNICAL PICTURE

We have spoken of the chart as a "picture," a picture of the composite evaluations going on in the minds of many people. We have spoken of the chart as "a tool." In spite of the possible effect of buying or selling by some technicians who use charts, we do not believe that "the chart makes the market go." On the contrary, we believe that the market makes its own complex evaluation, and the chart reflects this continually changing appraisal.

In general, as Charles H. Dow discovered before the turn of the century, the market tends to anticipate expected conditions. Therefore, (with Dow), we assume that when the market or some particular stock is moving strongly into higher ground, it is because people are anxious to buy it and are willing to bid more for it. Conversely, when a stock is slumping to new lows, it suggests that people are pessimistic about its future and are prepared to take less for it in order to get it off their hands.

This, as you will see, appears to run somewhat counter to the ordinary idea of buying something while it is cheap and selling it when it is dear. We read so often of stocks that are overpriced. Yet the man who sells these overpriced stocks, or sells them short, often finds that the Upward Trend continues for months or years. Similarly, the investor who attempts to buy at the bottom is often disappointed, since the stock which has been in trouble for some time is quite likely to continue to slump.

There is something else about the low-priced stocks that should be mentioned here. It seems reasonable to suppose that stock that once sold at $100 a share, which has dropped to $10 a share, must be at or near its ultimate bottom. An investor will sometimes argue that since it has already dropped 90 points from 100 to 10, it cannot drop more than 10 points at the most. But this is a trap and a very dangerous one. Consider that you have $10,000 to invest. This would have bought you 100 shares of the stock at the price of $100. When the stock dropped to 10, your accrued loss would have been 90% or $9,000. But if you should wait, and then buy the stock at $10, and it should drop 9 points to $1, your loss would have once again been 90%; and if you had used the same capital of $10,000 to buy 1,000 shares at $10, you would have suffered a loss of $9,000, the same as in the first case. On a percentage basis (which is what the logarithmic scales show clearly) there is no bottom to the chart, and no top—no limit to what portion of your capital you could make or lose.

Chapter 4:
The Importance of Trends

It almost always surprises novices to discover that on logarithmic charts the price moves so frequently lie along straight lines, forming "Trend Channels" that may run for months, or for years. For example, the long-term Uptrend in International Business Machines ran from the end of 1953 to the beginning of 1962; over eight years, in one straight Trend Channel so precise you could lay a steel ruler along it and it would not violate the upward sloping Trends at any point. Incidentally, when it did break this Trend, in January, 1962, the price dropped precipitously from over 600 to 300 in less than six months. The Trends of stocks normally move down faster than they move up.

Before one can buy or sell a stock, it is necessary to have some clear idea of what constitutes a change in the Trend, so that as far as possible, one will not be for long on the wrong side of the Major Trend.

It is easy to verify the existence of these straight-line Trends. It is easy to see that stocks do not ordinarily jump around in complete random fluctuations, but move in more or less orderly progression for considerable periods of time. However, knowing this does not automatically, and by itself, solve all problems. As a matter of fact, though it is worth knowing, it solves no problems. Before one can buy or sell a stock, it is necessary to have some clear idea of what constitutes a change in the Trend, so that as far as possible, one will not be for long on the wrong side of the Major Trend. This is a matter calling for the most intense observation and study. It may require auxiliary studies. (For example, the volume of trading times the price of a stock represents the number of dollars involved in the market action on a particular day. It makes a great difference whether the total trading amounted to $10,000 or $10,000,000.) As we said before, the chart is merely a tool, a means of setting down graphically some data about the market action.

HINDSIGHT AS A WORKING TOOL

A good many investors and traders give their entire attention to what is going on now in the market; not only in the market, but as to corporate affairs, national politics, international affairs, monetary conditions, etc. They are trying to interpret the present and estimate the probable future; but they are not well prepared to do this unless and until they have acquired some knowledge of the past. One of the most valuable study aids a technician can have is his file of stock charts for previous years. By studying how stocks have acted in the past, the typical action during booms and busts, the Bottom formations and Top patterns, the extent and duration of Trends, etc., he will be better prepared to evaluate a new situation. In fact, his intuition, his understanding of the market (which is in his mind, not in the chart) will develop as he acquires more experience, more understanding of what has happened in the past. The times may be different, the conditions may be different, the particular stock may be different from others that have been studied. And, yet, while history does not ever exactly repeat itself, one learns what seems most likely to happen under certain circumstances.

One of the most valuable study aids a technician can have is his file of stock charts for previous years.

This is like learning in any field. The surgeon, the lawyer, the musician, and the executive must continually face new problems not precisely like any encountered before. But he must have had the experience of analyzing other problems from the past that are in some significant ways similar. So that when he is confronted with an entirely new problem, he can draw on this storehouse of experience, and in "playing it by ear," put to use the intuitive knowledge he has gained from these past events.

We cannot make the point too strongly that chart interpretation and technical market wisdom is not learned overnight. We cannot stress too much the importance of looking back, and if one has noted his past opinions and evaluations on the charts (as he should, to get the most value from them), to check these out and see where his judgments were good, where they failed, and, if they failed, whether it seemed to be because of some correctable error in judgment or whether it was because of an unexpected and unpredictable change of conditions.

TRENDS, REVERSALS, CORRECTIONS AND CONSOLIDATIONS

If we are agreed that the chart is a valid representation of the daily price and volume action in the market, and if we agree that it is primarily the market that makes the charts go and not the chart that makes the market go, then we can regard the chart as a map of conditions that exist in the market.

So long was we keep it clearly in mind that our map, though accurate and correct in what it shows, does not show everything (no map shows everything in the territory it represents), we can deal with the chart (or map) in many ways as if it were the territory itself.

We will look for relations, but we must be careful not to attribute causes too freely. Quite often it is not necessary or possible to know the cause or causes of a market condition, even though we know very well there must be causes. It can be dangerous to pin causes on things. If, for example, we were to say the birds return in the spring and the leaves get green in the spring, that the leaves get green because the birds come back, we would be quite wrong. And we might dangerously confuse ourselves in giving weight to a cause-and-effect relationship between drug addicts and inferior abilities. One might assume that since inferior behavior and drug addiction are frequently found in association, therefore the drug addiction was the cause or reason for the inferior behavior in work, social relations, etc. Or, vice versa, we might assume that general incompetence and inferior abilities were the cause of addiction. This might indeed be a false lead that could confuse understanding of the problem. Better to treat relationships simply as relationships, without continually trying to pin a cause-and-effect label on the relations.

Analyzing Bar Charts for Profit

If we can take the chart as an abstraction, leaving causes and effects out of it, then we can see some relations that might otherwise be overlooked.

For example, the chart of a Utility stock may show a very definite technical pattern, let us say a Rectangular Horizontal Channel from which the price breaks away sharply upward on increased volume. *(See Chart A.)* We may, in fact we do, see other charts with almost identical patterns and behavior—steel stocks, oil stocks, motors, rubbers, etc. In fact, this particular type of market pattern may turn up in any type of stock at some time or other; or, for that matter, it may appear in bond charts, commodity charts, or in the charts of anything traded in a free competitive market.

Since the same type of pattern, with the same sort of breakout and similar consequences after the breakout, shows up again and again in many different kinds of market charts, we must conclude that the chart pattern is not a particular characteristic of railroads or steel companies, etc., but is more likely related to the dynamics of markets generally, or to be more specific, to the perceptive habits of people. In a sense, we are looking much more at the operation of men's minds than at the conditions affecting a corporation. Or, shall we say, if we are looking at the affairs of the corporation, we are seeing them "as perceived" by the buyers and sellers in the market, and it is that perception and evaluation that is recorded on the chart. The underlying reasons could be many. It is not actually necessary to inquire in detail what they are.

Again, you will find the same Trends and chart patterns on charts representing market action in 1989, and in those of 1979, or 1929, or 1889. An experienced technical trader today could be taken back in time 30 years; he could be confronted with stocks in a foreign market; and, if he were familiar with the typical behavior of stocks generally, as it is shown on the daily charts, he could draw some useful information from the charts. He might even operate better in such an unfamiliar market than some who are so close to it they "could not see the forest for the trees."

CHART A

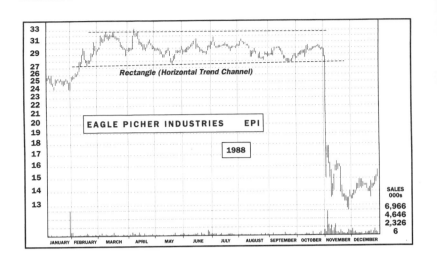

EAGLE PICHER INDUSTRIES—*Here we have a Rectangle (or, you might say, a Horizontal Trend Channel), moving between the limits of, roughly, 27 and 33. This is the type of trading action, or non-action, that requires considerable patience to follow. It is also a good example of why you should keep a close watch on stocks you own, even if they seem to be very stable. Notwithstanding the lengthy Consolidation period, one might have been more vigilant in watching pattern support in the October-November timeframe, since this was the anniversary of the spectacular 1987 crash, and apprehension in the stock market during this period was high that "the other shoe" would fall. Aside from the Breakout itself, which points to the direction of the expected move and signals the investor to either sell short or cover previous long positions, there was little warning that the Consolidation was at an end. But the extraordinary jump in volume on the Tuesday before the Wednesday Breakout (the second-largest volume of the year) was a clear indication that something was amiss. The decline was severe and, unlike the rest of the stock market, EPI did not recover. By the end of 1989, it was testing its 1982 low at 10.*

Analyzing Bar Charts for Profit

Let us consider a stock that has been selling in a dull sort of way, for a considerable time, at or near a certain price range. Suddenly, it comes to life. It advances sharply and on very much increased volume. It is possible that such a breakout may come about through a false rumor, a piece of gossip about the stock, or perhaps a premature "guess" that something is about to happen. If you felt that there was a good chance that such-and-such a company would get the big aircraft contract next month, or might be merged on favorable terms with one of its competitors, or was about to win an important lawsuit, you might well buy some of the stock; and if some others felt as you did, they might well be willing to pay a little more than the market price in order to get their shares. If there were enough eager buyers, this could use up all the available stock offered at the prices at which this stock had been selling and eventually force the bids considerably higher in order to attract sellers willing to part with some of their holdings.

Whether or not a particular breakout of this sort will be the beginning of a long and profitable advance depends on whether the original information was correct and whether the expected action takes place and other factors. But, when a big move in stock does take place, it is very like to emerge from just this kind of situation. If one is not too impetuous, does not jump in too heavily and risk too much, and if one is prepared to get out again, often with a loss in case the move fails, he is likely to pick up one of the important cases where a new Major Trend is getting under way.

However, it is all too common for an inexperienced trader to become nervous as his stock advances. Sometimes it seems he will suffer more when a stock is going his way than when it is moving against him. There seems to be a temptation to get out too soon, to "take profits," and, in fact, one of the oldest (and most misleading) market maxims is, "No man ever went broke taking a profit." While the statement is true, the implications of it are deceptive; for unless a man can stick with a strong stock as long as it remains strong, his losses may outweigh his gains.

One of the oldest (and most misleading) market maxims is, "no man ever went broke taking a profit."

It is best not to be too urgently anxious to get out of a profitable stock. If you will check the records of some dozens or hundreds of stocks, as shown on long-term monthly charts, you will find that the Major Trends do not switch from strong to weak and weak to strong every week or so. You will see very plainly that normally a well-established Trend in a stock continues for some time, that is to say, for months, sometimes for years. The upmoving stock is likely to continue to move up. The downmoving stock continues to slide.

Therefore, once we have determined or decided that a stock is in a Major Trend, if we have a position in that stock in line with the Trend, we should stay with it until there is some evidence that the stock is no longer moving in that Trend.

This is easier said than done, of course, since every stock has its daily fluctuations and is also subject to the general dips and rallies of the market as a whole. Nevertheless, it is possible to make some observations, to set up some rules of procedure, and, in time, to acquire a "method" based on observation and experience which will help in getting into stocks in line with their Major Trends and in getting out of these positions only when the Trend seems seriously threatened. Not only will one acquire a set of principles or rules of operation, but, more importantly, he will gradually get a feeling or intuition of the action of stocks as a result of having followed, observed, and tentatively judged many such actions in the past.

It is not possible to make a simple set of maxims or directives that can be used as a formula and which will absolutely prevent loss and ensure profits. The market is not that easy. Furthermore, each investor has his own objectives and philosophy. There are some who are interested only in short-term gains; they are temperamentally in-and-outers and do not feel at ease in a long-time holding. If they understand clearly that the problems of the short-time market trader are complicated by very high costs to cover the frequent commissions, transfer taxes, odd-lot fees, and unavoidable execution losses, and if they are prepared for the nerve-wracking, tense battle all day and every day, they may be able to hold their own in that small group of short-term traders who are successful on balance.

For most of us, the more profitable course lies in holding a stock position as long as it looks good and closing it out just as soon as it no longer seems tenable. This also requires courage and constant study, and, in addition, it requires the most difficult quality of all—the ability to sit and wait, sometimes for weeks or months. It calls for patience.

Whether one's plan is short-term trading or long-term, the investor must be prepared to accept losses, to forget what he paid for the stock, and deal with it according to its current action only, regardless of whether it shows him an accrued gain or loss at a given time.

CHANGES IN TREND CALL FOR CHANGES OF POSITION

Let us say we have taken a long position in a stock which has broken out of dormancy, as we described, such a situation above. We will assume that the stock has entered a Major Uptrend, and this Trend will be considered in effect until such time as there are indications that convince us that the Trend has been broken decisively.

This, of course, is easy to say and much harder to do. The whole science or art of technical analysis of stock trends is involved here, and it depends a great deal on the individual skill, experience, and perception of the investor as to how well he will do. It also depends on whether he has the conviction and courage to follow and carry out with determination the decisions his method lead to.

Finally, it calls for a realistic understanding that, in spite of the most careful, most intelligent study of a stock situation, there is still a considerable area of uncertainty. No one can make predictions with anything like absolute certainty. If he is satisfied his method and original basis of decision were correct, if the situation changes greatly, he must be prepared to face the fact that some new conditions have arisen, and he must act accordingly. It is no reflection on his method that he should have to revise his opinion or reverse his decision in light of new

The more profitable course lies in holding a stock position as long as it looks good and closing it out just as soon as it no longer seems tenable. This also requires courage and constant study, and, in addition, it requires the most difficult quality of all—the ability to sit and wait sometimes for weeks or months. It calls for patience.

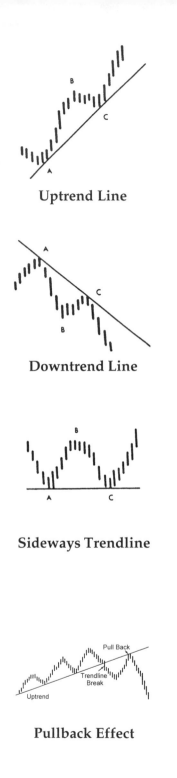

Uptrend Line

Downtrend Line

Sideways Trendline

Pullback Effect

facts. One of the most damaging, sometimes ruinous, points of view is that of the man who is so "wedded" to his original conclusion that he cannot face the fact that the situation is different this month from what it may have been three months ago.

FOLLOWING THE TREND

There are almost as many definitions of a Trend as there are investors to make them. Normally, the Trend of a stock is a more or less irregular affair, with bursts of high volume as new peaks are reached, and then periods of a few days or a few weeks with shrinking volume of trading, followed by another advance on increasing volume. Some setbacks may be very short and of limited extent—a few days or a week, perhaps. Others, especially after a series of minor advances, may be of greater extent and may last for a number of weeks or several months. Yet all of these may fit into the main or Major Uptrend.

No method of determining whether or not the Major Trend is still in effect is infallible. However, there are a number of methods of estimating whether or not an important change of Trend has occurred.

The simplest of these is to draw a Trendline, that is to say, a line which touches the Bottoms of two or more reactions if the Major Trend is up. (In the case of downmoving stocks, the Trendline would be drawn across the Tops of two or more rallies.) In many cases the Trend will follow a straight line, especially on logarithmically scaled charts, and a sharp breakdown through the Trendline will dramatically underscore the change of Trend.

A case in point would be the long-term Trend in International Business Machines. After more than eight years of following a perfectly straight Trendline, IBM broke through that line in January, 1962, and by the end of May had dropped several hundred points. However, after that 1962 correction, IBM resumed the long-term Trendline through 1989.

In spite of the clear evidence that Trends do exist and that they follow straight lines on logarithmic charts, the simple Trendline is not by any means the whole answer to stock analysis—far from it. It is not always easy or possible to find clear points of reference through which to draw the Trendline. Quite frequently, the chart will show a sideways movement that will penetrate the Trendline without volume or any substantial decline. It is necessary to understand that the way in which the Trendline is broken may be as important, or more important, than the fact it is broken. *(See Chart B.)*

It is necessary to understand that the way in which the Trendline is broken may be as important, or more important, than the fact it is broken.

In order to get around the difficulties of dealing with simple Trendlines, there have been various refinements and alternatives developed. Some technicians require a breakdown that penetrates the line by a definite minimum amount, say 3% or 5% of the price of the stock. Others will use double Trendlines, forming a channel that will include a warning area between a slight penetration and a full-scale signal. Some will use instead of the ordinary Trendline, a moving average, which may be based on the performance over any preceding period of time; we have 10-day moving averages, 30-day moving averages, 100-day and 200-day moving averages, etc. This tends to stabilize the picture and eliminate certain types of false or trivial moves, but it also introduces some other problems peculiar to moving averages. There have been methods in which two moving averages, a short-term and a longer-term one are used together to give indications of change of Trend when they cross. There are a number of other methods using Trendlines, moving averages, and some other devices to catch early signs of a Major turn.

Although none of these methods is entirely satisfactory, any of them is better than no method at all. They may not catch the exact or optimum point at which a decision could best be made, but they will at least ensure that an investor who follows them will not allow himself indefinitely to hold a stock that is piling up losses for him after a Major Reversal.

CHART B

ADVANCED MICRO DEVICES INC.—*Stocks tend to make straight-line Trends, either up, down, or horizontally. The Trends do not necessarily move in the same direction as "the average" or "the general market." Here, for example, we see a strong Downtrend in a particular stock at a time when the "general market" was moving sideways to higher. From June to December, AMD declined by nearly 50% in the face of a generally Bullish Market. Although this issue did enjoy a rally back to 11 during the first half of 1989, the Downtrend resumed the following June while the "averages" were challenging old highs. You will find some issues moving sharply higher in Bear Markets and others, like AMD, moving down in Bull Markets. This type of action does not strike us as "random." Apparently, some economic or psychological factors were operating to affect public opinion. But it is not necessary for the market technician to know what these factors may have been. The chart speaks for itself.*

Analyzing Bar Charts for Profit

There are other indications of turn and some suggest a Continuation of the Major Trend. The latter we have called Consolidation patterns. The former we call Reversal patterns.

In many cases, the Consolidation patterns in their early stages, look exactly like the Reversal patterns in their early stages (See Chart C). In fact, they probably arise from the same cause. When a stock has advanced in a strongly Bullish move for a time (or declined in a Bearish move), there will come a day when traders will decide to take profits (if they are on the right side of the stock), and what frequently occurs after a very rapid price move is a great increase of activity culminating in a burst of tremendously increased volume.

In the final day of a fast advance, the price may open on a "Gap," higher than the top price of the day before, and may go into entirely new high ground in the morning but then slump off as the day wears on, closing at or near the low for the day's trading. Such a climax day or One-Day Reversal is quite commonly the peak, the end of the advance for the time being. Following it, there may be a few days, a week or so, or a number of weeks, of decline or at least of inconsequential sideways movement, and this period will usually be marked by irregularly shrinking volume.

Whether or not the One-Day Reversal will prove to be of more than minor importance or not, we cannot tell at this stage, although many highwater marks preceding a severe Bear Market have been made on exactly this sort of day.

What seems more important here is that the One-Day Reversal, or, at any rate, a climax day of high volume, is likely to mark the end of one phase of an advance.

In any stock that is moving up (and what we say here would apply in reverse for downmoving stocks, of course), there are likely to be fairly frequent periods of correction or Consolidation, not necessarily, however, marking the ultimate end of the Major Trend.

The One-Day Reversal, or at any rate, a climax day of high volume, is likely to mark the end of one phase of an advance.

CHART C

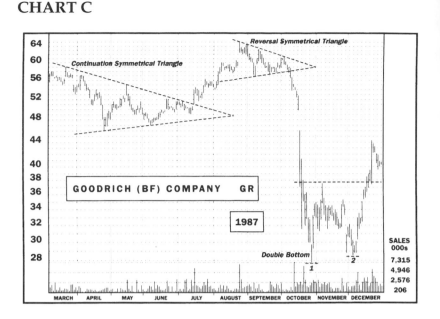

B.F. GOODRICH COMPANY—*Not only can chart patterns be described in several ways (see ASARCO), many can be either Reversal or Continuation patterns. The GR chart shows two unusually good examples, quite close together, of the dual nature of some chart patterns. After moving steadily higher in 1986 and early 1987, this issue turned sideways. From April through July, we see a series of advances and declines which all together add up to a narrowing Symmetrical Triangle. In mid-July, on sharply higher volume, GR broke out of the pattern to resume its previous Uptrend. Using the width of the pattern as a measure, you would have anticipated a move to the 63 area and not been disappointed when GR peaked in early September around 64 1/2. This is a Symmetrical Triangle as a Continuation pattern. Following the September peak, another series of fluctuations emerged, also taking the shape of a Symmetrical Triangle. This time, the decisive breakout was contra to the prevailing Uptrend, illustrating a Reversal Symmetrical Triangle. Notice the excellent Double Bottom which formed on the December test of the October low. The late December rally through 37, on rising volume, was a clear signal that the Downtrend was over. During the next two years, GR rallied to 70.*

A very common type of Consolidation occurs where the stock goes into a narrow horizontal range, moving, for example, from 32 to 36, and fluctuating back and forth within these limits in moves that may last a few days to a week or so. Ordinarily, as this Rectangle forms on the chart, the volume tends to shrink, although in a Bullish Trend, the peaks of the rallies may be marked by somewhat increased volume. In time, the stock will emerge from the Rectangle, and if this is an upside breakout, it will almost certainly be on greatly increased volume and will be quite unmistakable. Such a breakout suggests (a) that the Major Uptrend is still in effect and that further advances are probable, and (b) that there is likely to be an influx of Support (buying) on any reaction to the neighborhood of the Top of the Rectangle. In a Major Downtrend we also see Rectangles with similar characteristics except that volume on the downside moves or breakouts may not be so emphatically marked.

Rectangles are among the most beautiful and most interesting of the technical formations that appear on charts. They may be either Consolidations (or Continuation patterns) or they may mark an important turn (Reversal pattern). During their formation, it is not possible to say whether they mark a Consolidation or a Reversal; but on the basis that a Major Trend must be assumed to be in effect until there is clear evidence of Reversal, the presumption is that they are Consolidations until there is a contrary breakout. As a matter of fact, the majority of Rectangles, Symmetrical Triangles, etc., do turn out to be Consolidations.

A good example of a Rectangle as shown on a chart is to be seen in the 1988-1989 BankAmerica chart *(See Chart D)*.

You could regard Rectangles as "Horizontal Trend Channels," with tentative Trendlines drawn across the Tops and Bottoms.

When a breakout from such a pattern occurs, it is quite common to see the move run a few days and then return to approximately the breakout level before resuming the primary move.

CHART D

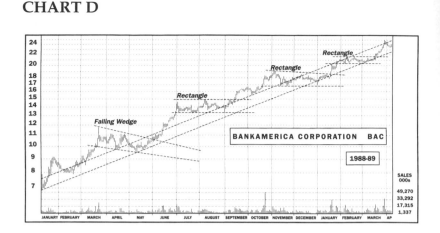

BANKAMERICA CORPORATION—*There are those who will tell us that the movements of stocks are as completely random as the stumblings of a drunk in a public square late at night, or as meaningless as the scores of a blindfolded dart player. Anyone who has kept daily charts of stocks knows that the charts do not provide "all the answers" nor do they infallibly "predict the future." But it is hard to believe that the Trends such as the Uptrend shown here in Bank-America or the Uptrend and Downtrend in Advanced Micro Devices could be the result of the gyrations of a drunk or the scores of a blindfolded dart player. In the BankAmerica chart you will also notice two other typical patterns, the Falling Wedge and Rectangle. The first is considered a Bullish pattern, and Confirmation is given when the upper boundary line is decisively broken on increasing volume. Rectangles, on the other hand, can be Continuation or Reversal patterns, depending on which way they break out of the formation. Generally speaking, Rectangles define a tug of war between two groups of approximately equal strength. The stock will bounce back and forth, trading within two horizontal boundary lines, until one side or the other is exhausted. The measuring implication of this pattern, that is, the expected minimum movement after the breakout, is the width of the Rectangle. A Rectangle 2-points wide, for example, should move at least 2 points beyond its breakout point.*

This raises the interesting point of Support and Resistance phenomena. When a stock has made a dynamic breakout move, this move is likely to be followed by some quick profit-taking; and a reaction will set in. However, it is believed by many observers that prospective buyers who may have missed the original breakout may then come into the market on the reaction. It is this buying that constitutes the Support that so frequently appears at or near the Bottoms of Rectangles (or in Bearish moves, the Resistance that appears at or near the Bottom of Rectangles).

There is another type of market action that is somewhat similar to the Rectangle. This has the form of a more or less Symmetrical Triangle, and we call it by that name. It is marked, usually, by a heavy volume climax as it goes into its first turning point; and this is followed by a series of declines and rallies which, instead of forming two parallel lines, as is the case of the Rectangles, tend to narrow, so that the lines drawn across the turning points will make a down-sloping and up-sloping side to the Triangle. It is a "narrowing" formation, ordinarily accompanied by shrinking volume, and is, in fact, both an Up-trend and a Downtrend at the same time (until it is broken). The Triangle may eventually turn into a Rectangle. More often it will break out decisively at some point well before it reaches the apex or intersection of its two bounding Trendlines. (See Chart E.)

The Symmetrical Triangles often mark important Consolidations and sometimes important Reversals. They are more subject to false moves than Rectangles, as when the price makes an "end run" entirely around the apex of the Triangle and reverses the move entirely.

An interesting feature of the Symmetrical Triangle is the market tendency of reactions after an emphatic breakout to return to the point of intersection of the two sides of the Triangle—the "cradle point" as Robert D. Edwards has called it.

With both the Rectangles and Symmetrical Triangles there is little indication of which way the breakout will occur. There is, however, another family of Triangles which carries a very

When a stock has made a dynamic breakout move, this move is likely to be followed by some quick profit-taking; and a reaction will set in.

CHART E

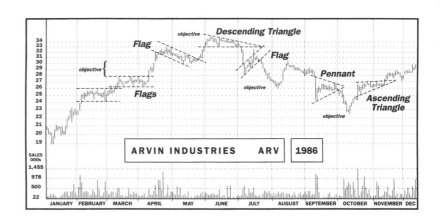

ARVIN INDUSTRIES—*In a strong up or down move, you will often see a series of Continuation patterns lead the stock higher or lower. Arvin provides an example of both an Uptrend and a Downtrend. In February, a four-week sideways pattern, which would be a Rectangle or a Flag, was broken on the upside restarting the January-February advance. An interesting feature of these small Continuation patterns is the fact that they offer measurement possibilities. Rectangle Breakouts usually will move the width of the pattern, but Flags frequently mark the midpoint of the move. In this case, a rally to the 28-30 level was suggested. Another Flag-Rectangle emerged which indicated the advance would carry to at least 30. The rally peaked at 33 in late April and pulled back for four weeks, forming another Bull Flag. This Breakout measured a move to the 36 area, which was not quite reached at the 35 high in June. The fact that AR fell short of its objective, however, was a sign that the Uptrend was running out of gas. The next four-week Consolidation was a small Descending Triangle (a Reversal pattern) completed in late June on a penetration of pattern support. Now the Bears took over and the July Flag, when broken, pointed to a decline to the 26 area. Through September, another variation of a Continuation pattern, the Pennant, can be seen. The Breakout of this pattern indicated a move to the 22 area. Once again, the failure to reach 22, although it did come close, was a sign that the Downtrend was near exhaustion. This Downtrend was, in fact, a Major correction in the long-term Uptrend which began in late 1982 around 6; over the next year, AR rallied to 40.*

definite indication of the probable move to come. These Triangles are known as Ascending Triangles (in which the successive minor peaks are at substantially the same price level and the successive Bottoms are at continually higher levels) and Descending Triangles (in which the Minor Bottoms come at about the same price level but successive rallies Top out at continually lower levels). *(See Charts F and G.)* The Ascending Triangle *(See Chart H)* apparently corresponds to a Resistance level (or supply level), and the successively Rising Bottoms show the tendency of investors to be willing to pay more for the stock on its declines. The reverse would be true of the Descending Triangle *(See Chart F)*. So, these types of Triangle patterns can normally be regarded as Bullish (for the ascending type) and normally Bearish (for the descending type). In some cases, these patterns, like all chart patterns, will fail and even when they do not completely fail, they are often prone to turning into Rectangles as time goes on. But all in all, the Ascending and Descending Triangles are among the most dependable of chart patterns.

The question of measurement is bound to come up in connection with chart formations. It is not possible to make very accurate estimates as to how far a move will go. At best, one can state a minimum probable move, but we would not consider a stock which has made such a minimum probable move and has reached it estimated objective should be sold. If the move is part of a Major Trend, the advance may continue far beyond the objective and there is no guarantee, in any case, that a particular target will be reached. We would use any measuring formulas as guides or auxiliary information, but we would not hold to them as to a religion.

In general, we assume that the probable move out of a pattern, such as the Rectangles, Symmetrical Triangles, and Ascending and Descending Triangles, will be at least equal to the measurement of the pattern on its first "leg." In the case of the Rectangles, this would mean the measurement from Top to Bottom. With the Triangles, it would be the same distance as the "open side" of the Triangle.

All in all, the Ascending and Descending Triangles are among the most dependable of chart patterns.

CHART F

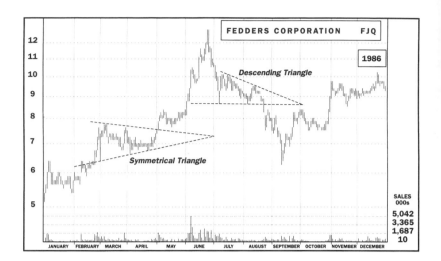

FEDDERS USA INC.—*Here is the typical Symmetrical Triangle in which a stock goes into a series of fluctuations which gradually narrow down as though the stock has (for the time being) stabilized. A decisive breakout, either up or down, is likely to point to the direction of the next significant move. In this case, FJQ broke out of a 9-week Triangle on the upside. This was a clear signal of what was likely to follow. Notice the rise in volume on the breakout. Without the increased trading activity, the breakout would have been suspect. However, on a Downside Breakout, an increase in trading volume is not required to validate it; stocks can fall of their own weight. You can observe this by looking at the breakout of the Descending Triangle which formed below the June peak in July and August. On the decisive penetration of pattern support, and the subsequent 3-week decline, volume was light and well below activity found on the rally of those days where it did increase.*

CHART G

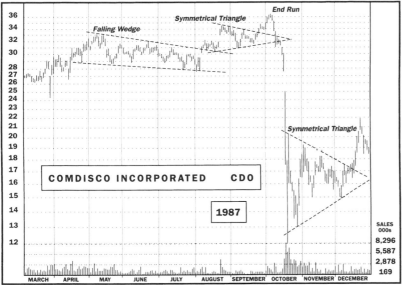

COMDISCO INC.—*It is not always possible to make an "overperfect" picture of a technical situation. There may be premature and/or false breakouts to cloud the picture. End runs are also a hazard. This, of course, is why we employ stop-loss protection. Here, we see several examples of false breakouts, and an end run, on the same chart. Beginning in April, CDO began to fluctuate sideways in a narrowing, but slightly downward-slanting pattern. Initially, several formations were possible. But, as the Consolidation stretched out into July, it took the shape of a Falling Wedge. This is a Bullish pattern, so an upside breakout would be expected. Notice that in late July, however, Support was broken. This would have called for some special attention, but it did not go far outside the boundary of the Wedge before pulling back into the formation. It happened in early August as well, but, again, the break was not decisive and the close in both cases was basically on the boundary line. These two breakouts were false. The true breakout came shortly thereafter on a high-volume rally through the upper boundary line. CDO turned sideways again forming an excellent Symmetrical Triangle on diminishing volume. In late September, it broke out of the Triangle on the upside. The rally stalled a week later, and prices plunged back through Triangle Support on heavy volume—a clear failure of the breakout which "has aptly been termed an end run around the line." CDO formed a large Symmetrical Triangle after the crash and broke to the upside in early December, retracing most of its October loss over the next two years.*

CHART H

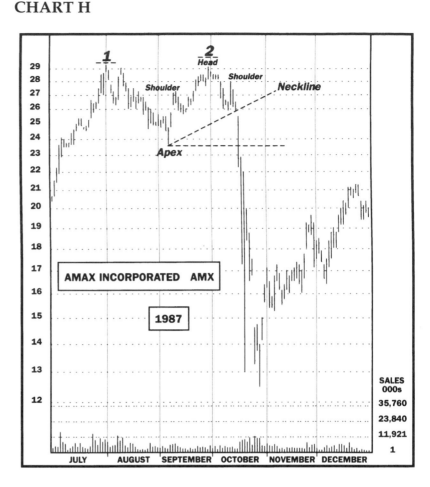

AMAX INC.—*This is a very good example of a Double Top formation. There is probably no technical pattern that is more abused than the Double Top, along with the Double Bottom. Actually, the formation calls for a peak, usually on increased volume, followed by a sagging "valley" with reduced volume activity. A final attempt to rally, again with no great volume, occurs which fails to get substantially above the previous Top. The completion of the Double Top, however, calls for a decisive breakdown through the Bottom of the valley between the two peaks, which should be at least a month apart to separate the Tops from being a part of the same Consolidation. The Double Top in AMAX was confirmed on the Friday preceding the October 19, 1987 crash in the stock market. Interestingly, a small Head-and-Shoulders Top pattern developed on the rally, forming the*

CHART H
(Continued)

AMAX INC. (Continued)—*second Top. The Double Top was the larger and more dominant formation, but the penetration of the Head-and-Shoulders Neckline, also on Friday, gave a slightly higher signal to be out of, or short, this issue. Although deep, the October decline in AMAX (and the stock market) proved to be short lived. But, the fine Ascending Triangle which emerged during November, and the subsequent breakout at 17 1/2, was an excellent rebuy point. In Double Bottoms, the reverse criteria would apply: two Bottoms, with an intervening rally, and finally a clear upside penetration of the rally Top, accompanied by a considerable increase in volume of trading. Just as the Double Top strongly suggests a Downside move in the making, the Double Bottom, when completed, points toward a probable advance (see Goodrich Chart).*

There is another type of Continuation pattern that should be mentioned here. Normally, it is a Consolidation or Continuation pattern and it is frequently found in the charts of stocks that are making a very large and rapid move either up or down. We will speak, here, of the upmoving case; but the downmoving is quite similar, in reverse.

The patterns we are speaking of occur after a rapid, almost vertical advance, oftentimes a move that may "Gap" from day to day and which may cover many points in a week or in two weeks' time. There may be a One-Day Reversal at the end of such a "leg" in a move, or there may not. But the stock is quite likely, in any case, to "stall," decline, and then, with volume shrinking sharply, to go into a tight, narrow pattern as seen on the chart, like a Flag or Pennant which may be flying horizontally or may be drooping somewhat. If anyone seeks an explanation of this sudden halt and Consolidation, he may well regard this as a period of profit-taking by quick-turn speculators or the rather premature selling out of investors who are over eager to take profits. It will, undoubtedly, represent, too, the trading of those who hope to sell the stock near a temporary Top and then buy in on the first reaction. *(See Chart I.)*

In any case, such a pattern is not to be regarded as Bearish. It normally suggests the likelihood of a powerful resumption of the move in the near future. Although, as with all market phenomena, this is not a certainty, the rewards of patience during the Flag- and Pennant-type corrections are often richly worth exercising that patience.

Schabacker has stated that Flags and Pennants *(See Charts G, J and K)* carry a rather definite measuring implication, namely, that the Continuation of the move after a breakout from the Flag or Pennant is likely to measure about as much as the original fast move leading into the pattern; or, as he put it, "The flag flies at half-mast." It is extraordinary how often this particular measurement is completed. But, in such a case, we would not feel that after the attainment of the objective the stock should be sold. For it can go into another Continuation pattern and then break out again for still further advances.

CHART I

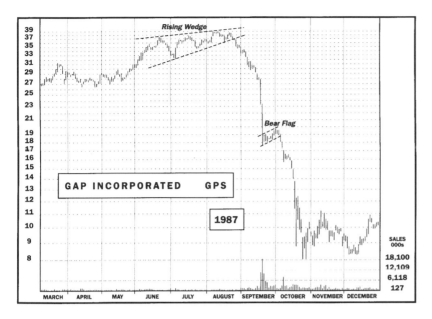

GAP INCORPORATED—*GPS was a spectacular performer in the decade of the 1980s. From under a 1 in 1980, this issue exceeded 76 at its 1987 peak. Along the way, it also suffered some substantial setbacks. To look at a long-term chart (monthly), these downturns look as if they materialized out of thin air. While it is true that stocks can reverse dramatically when some sort of fundamental news hits everyone by surprise, like a particularly well-kept takeover attempt, or a disaster like the gas leak in Bhopal, India, which hurt Union Carbide, more often than not, signs of a change of direction will show up in the daily chart. In GPS, for example, it was hard to miss the deteriorating technical position which occurred through the summer of 1987. Oscillating higher, on generally weakening volume, (note that each high from June on occurred on lower volume), GPS formed a fine Rising Wedge pattern. Just opposite of the Falling Wedge (see Comdisco chart), this pattern has Bearish implications. Well before the rest of the market collapsed, Comdisco (CDO) had fallen through Support and was heading sharply lower. An excellent Bear Flag, evident at the end of September, was also completed before the October crash in the general market.*

CHART J

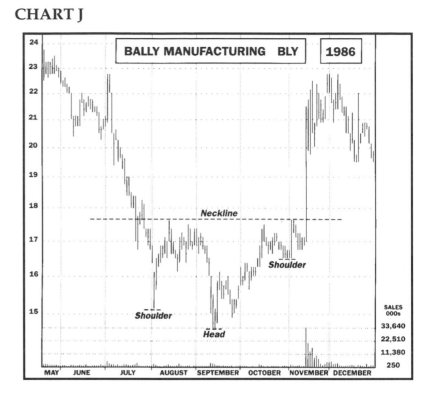

BALLY MANUFACTURING CORPORATION—*Since the Head-and-Shoulders Top takes place during a period of enthusiasm, in a stock that has been leaping forward, typically, there is a great amount of activity as it is transferred from "strong hands" to "weak hands." On the other hand, the Head-and-Shoulders Bottom occurs after a series of discouraging collapses, at a time when there is less enthusiasm to buy the stock and when it is mostly neglected. So, a resurgence of volume is most important to validate any important Bottom pattern. Volume represents dollars. Twice as much volume means twice as many dollars and is, therefore, twice as important. Notice the volume increase as BLY comes out of its slump. This Reversal was the start of an advance which carried Bally to 28 before the 1987 decline.*

Analyzing Bar Charts for Profit

CHART K

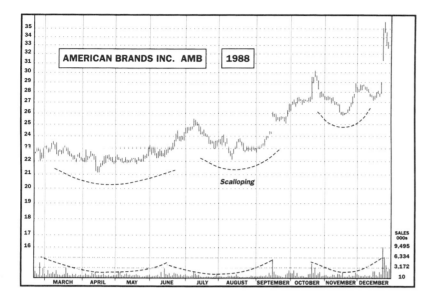

AMERICAN BRANDS INC. AMB   1988

Scalloping

SALES
000s
9,495
6,334
3,172
10

MARCH APRIL MAY JUNE JULY AUGUST SEPTEMBER OCTOBER NOVEMBER DECEMBER

AMERICAN BRANDS INC.—*Stocks in which there is at all times a fairly active market with a large number of shares outstanding will sometimes make long advances in a series of Saucers. "These successive patterns, each of which resembles in both price and volume, the action of the Rounding Bottom, are slightly up-tilted. That is, the rising end always carries prices a little higher than the preceding Top at the beginning of the Saucer." AMB is a particularly fine example of this phenomenon which is called Scalloping. Reactions from the lefthand lip of each Saucer or Scallop tend to run in the 20% to 30% area while advances will exceed 15% or more of the price of the stock. Notice the Breakaway Gaps in September and December. By late 1989, this issue was trading over 80.*

There are a number of other technical patterns, Trend actions, Support and Resistance phenomena, etc., which might be studied, but which would require an entire book to deal with adequately.

However, there is one particular chart picture which is of such prime importance that we have saved discussion of it for the last.

This is the Head-and-Shoulders pattern which can appear at both Tops and Bottoms, and which is a major indication of Reversal, which has appeared in the charts of dozens or hundreds of stocks during every important market Top or Bottom. *(See Chart L.)*

This pattern was observed and discussed in connection with stock averages by Charles H. Dow and William Peter Hamilton over half a century ago. It was studied extensively by Richard W. Schabacker and was explained in considerable detail by Humphrey B. Neil in his fine book, *Tape Reading and Market Tactics,* some sixty years ago.

The Head-and-Shoulders Top *(See Chart C)* in its simplest form consists of the next to last and the final rallies in a Major Uptrend, the first (failing) rally of a Major Downtrend, and the penetration of the "Neckline" marking the Bottoms between the rallies.

Typically, a stock, and often an average, will follow a Major Trend in a series of waves, that is to say, advances interrupted by corrective reactions. This has been compared to the advance of the incoming tide on a beach, not steadily, but in a series of advancing highwater points as the breakers wash higher and higher up the sands. When the succession of large waves begins to fall short of a highwater mark, and the intervening ebb runs back to a lower point, one can infer that "the tide has turned." It is a good analogy.

The Head-and-Shoulders Top is normally marked, like most technical patterns, by unusually high volume on the "left shoulder." The "Head," which goes to a new high on the price

When the succession of large waves begins to fall short of a highwater mark, and the intervening ebb runs back to a lower point, one can infer that "the tide has turned."

Analyzing Bar Charts for Profit

CHART L

DILLARD DEPARTMENT STORES INC. DDS

1987

SALES 000s
5,695
3,783
1,907
31

MAY   JUNE   JULY   AUGUST   SEPTEMBER   OCTOBER   NOVEMBER   DECEMBER

DILLARD DEPARTMENT STORES INC.—*This is a Head-and-Shoulders Top. The Head-and-Shoulders patterns, Top and Bottom, are the most well-known of the classical charts; they are also the most reliable of the Major Reversal patterns. Here, the price action traces the Head-and-Shoulders very clearly, breaking away on the downside with an open Gap. During what proved to be the 1987 peak in the "averages" in August and September, a significant number of individual stocks, like DDS, were clearly showing topping activity. The actual breakdown in the stock market in October, therefore, was not surprising; only the speed and the depth of the collapse were. It should be noted, however, that stocks almost always go down faster than they go up. Except for takeover situations, you will make money quicker on the short side of the market than the long side. Indeed, it took Dillard four months to drop from roughly 58 to 24; it took 17 months to recoup the loss. This Head-and-Shoulders Top exhibits the typical volume characteristics of the pattern—higher trading volume on the Left Shoulder than the Head, and relatively flat volume on the Right Shoulder. The penetration of the Neckline showed higher volume, but would also be valid on low volume as long as it were broken by 3%.*

scale, will ordinarily have less volume accompanying it. The (lower) "right shoulder" is usually made on relatively low volume.

The Neckline of such a pattern appears to represent good Support, and until and unless it is broken, it is probably best not to try to jump the gun by assuming the Head-and-Shoulders will be completed by such a breakthrough. When a Neckline breakdown happens, it may be on increased volume or it may not. However, such a break, even though it merely drifts through the Neckline on very small volume, should not be taken lightly. If it has substantially broken the Neckline (say by 3% of the price of the stock), it is likely to indicate a serious situation.

Such a break, even though it merely drifts through the Neckline on very small volume, should not be taken lightly.

After such a break, there may be a rally. Although there is no promise or certainty of such a rally, it does occur in many, and, perhaps, a majority of cases. But this rally will usually get no further than the general level of the Neckline, and the drop-off from here is likely to be precipitous and on greater volume.

The question can be asked, "how much of a decline might one expect after a definite Head-and-Shoulders break?" The most that one can be fairly definite of expecting is a decline amounting to the height of the pattern itself; that is to say, the height from the top of the Head to the Neckline will represent the minimum expected drop from the point of penetration of the Neckline.

The comment may very well be made that this is not such a great drop; and that if this is all there is to it, it might be best to hold the stock or even buy it on the decline. This, however, is not the whole story. When a Major Uptrend has been in effect for a long time, say six months or a year or more, and then a pattern of this sort appears, either a Head-and-Shoulders, a large Descending Triangle, or a long Rectangle broken on the downside, this may indicate a change in the Major Trend. There is a presumption, or at least a suspicion, that the successive rallies will come lower and lower and that the stock may plunge in a series of drops that may far exceed the minimum implications of the original Top formation. We would never disregard a clearly formed and definitely broken Head-and-Shoulders Top or any other typical Top patterns.

We have spoken about the simple Head-and-Shoulders Top, but you will find that there are many minor variations of this. There may be a Double Head, there may be two or more left shoulders at about the same height, or two or more right shoulders. In the case of slow-moving, large-issue investment stocks, this type of pattern may become a Rounding Top, *(See Chart K),* having few, if any, definite rallies and declines, but with the general picture of heavy upside volume gradually petering out, and then increasing again as the stock "rounds over" and starts its Downtrend.

In the case of Head-and-Shoulders Bottoms *(See Chart M),* the situation is similar, but reversed. The formation is "upside down" and some writers have referred to it as a Pendant Bottom. Here, we have the heavy volume on the left shoulder, a rally, then a further drop to a new low (the Head), and a recovery move that is likely to be marked by somewhat more volume than we have seen on a rally for some time. A corrective reaction on low volume takes the stock part way down again (right shoulder), and then a sharp advance occurs (which must be on heavy volume), smashing through the Neckline defined by the two previous minor rallies.

The main differences between the Head-and-Shoulders Tops and Bottoms are (a) the Top formations are often completed in a few weeks, whereas, a Major Bottom of any sort usually takes longer, and, in some cases, may cover from several months to a year and a half; and (b) the breakout move from Head-and-Shoulders Top formations may not be marked by much increase in volume, whereas, the breakout from the Head-and-Shoulders Bottom must have volume confirmation.

In concluding this discussion of daily charts and their use, we would once more like to emphasize that the chart is merely a map of what the market is doing and the market action is a composite of what people are thinking about a stock or about the market. There is no magic to a chart picture. It is a visual aid to the investor's thinking. In the final analysis, his success

CHART M

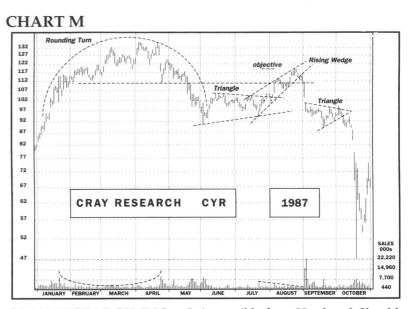

CRAY RESEARCH INC.—*It is possible for a Head-and-Shoulders to have multiple parts, i.e., two right shoulders, two heads, two left shoulders. These formations are called Complex Head-and-Shoulders patterns. However, if you carry this process out far enough, these complexes sometimes merge into Reversals known as Rounding Turns. Rounding Turns picture "simply and plainly, a gradual, progressive, and fairly symmetrical change in the Trend direction produced by a gradual shift in the balance of power between buying and selling." Bottoms are referred to as Bowl or Saucer patterns while Tops are sometimes called Inverted Bowls. Neither type, however, appears as often as Head-and-Shoulders formations. Tops, moreover, are rare in lower- and medium-priced stocks, but are found more often in higher-priced issues. CYR is a fine example of a Top. Volume on Bottoms is more subdued and forms a Bowl pattern along with the price. Volume on Tops is not as clean-cut and decisive, but will also have a Bowl or concave shape as well. After turning lower in late May, CRAY turned sideways to higher, from June to early September, pulling back through old Support (now new Resistance) at 112—once broken, a Support or Resistance line reverses function. A narrow Triangle emerged which was broken on the upside in early August. The width of the pattern indicated a minimum objective of 119 which turned out to be the high point of the rally. While a Reversal might have been suspected on the initial breakout of the Triangle, the diminishing volume on the advance, combined with converging Uptrend lines forming a Rising Wedge, were clearly Bearish.*

will depend in large part on his own powers of abstraction, observation, and ability to follow in practice the decisions he has arrived at in his mind. Continual study and review, back-checking on previous decisions and their consequences, experimentation and trial and error cannot help but build confidence, eliminate mistakes in trading, and improve one's practical ability to cope with the market.

Chapter 5:
Trend Channels

At the start of this Trend study, we applied the term *basic Trendline* to the line which slopes up across the wave Bottoms in an advance, and to the line which slopes down across the wave Tops in a decline. And we noted that the opposite Reversal points, i.e., the wave crests in an advance and the wave troughs in a decline, were, as a rule, less clearly delimited. That is one of the reasons why all of our discussion up to this point has been devoted to basic Trendlines. Another reason is, of course, that the technician's most urgent task is to determine when a Trend has run out and, for that purpose, the basic line is all-important.

In a fair share of normal Trends, however, the Minor waves are sufficiently regular to be defined at their other extremes by another line. That is, the *Tops* of the rallies composing an Intermediate advance sometimes develop along a line which is approximately parallel to the basic Trendline projected along their Bottoms. This parallel might be called the *return line* since it marks the zone where reactions (return moves against the prevailing Trend) originate. The area between basic Trendline and return line is the *Trend Channel*.

Nicely defined Trend Channels appear most often in actively traded stocks of large outstanding issue—least often in the less popular and the relatively thin equities which receive only sporadic attention from investors. The value of the Trend Channel concept for the technical trader would hardly seem to require extended comment.

Its greatest utility, however, is not what usually appeals to the beginner when he first makes its acquaintance, viz., the determination of good profit-taking levels. Experienced technicians, rather, find it more helpful in a negative sense. Thus, once a Trend Channel appears to have become well established, any failure of a rally to reach the return line (top parallel of the Channel in an Intermediate advance) is taken as a sign of deterioration of the Trend. Further, the margin by which a rally fails to reach the return line (before turning down) frequently equals the margin by which the basic Trendline is penetrated by the ensuing decline before a halt or throwback in the latter occurs.

By the same token, given an established Trend Channel, when a reaction from the return line fails to carry prices all the way back to the basic Trendline, but bottoms out somewhere above it, the advance from that Bottom will usually push up out of the Channel on the top side (through the return line) by a margin approximately equal to the margin by which the reaction failed to reach the Bottom of the Channel (basic Trendline).

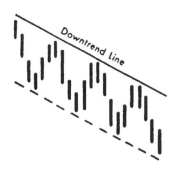

Downtrend Channel

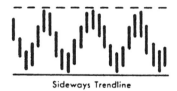

Sideways Channel

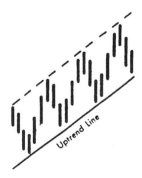

Uptrend Channel

Chapter 6:
Gaps

A Gap in the language of the chart technician represents a price range at which (at the time it occurred) no shares changed hands. This is a useful concept to keep in mind, because it helps to explain some of their technical consequences.

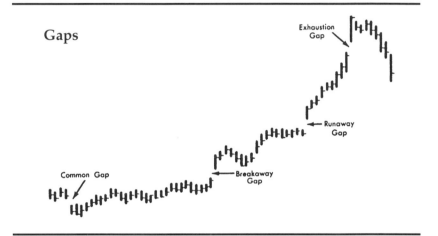

Gaps

Exhaustion Gap

Runaway Gap

Breakaway Gap

Common Gap

Gaps on daily charts are produced when the *lowest* price at which a certain stock is traded on any one day is *higher* than the *highest* price at which it was traded on the preceding day. Or when the highest price of one day is lower than the lowest price of the preceding day. When the ranges of any two such days are plotted, they will not overlap or touch the same horizontal level on the chart. There will be a price Gap between them. For a Gap to develop on a weekly chart it is necessary that the lowest price recorded at any time in one week be higher than the highest recorded during any day of the preceding week. This can happen, of course, and does, but, for obvious reasons, not as often as daily Gaps. Monthly chart Gaps are rare in actively traded issues; their occurrence is confined almost entirely to those few instances where a panic decline commences just before the end of a month and continues through the first part of the succeeding month.

THE COMMON OR AREA GAP

This type of Gap gets its name from its tendency to occur within a trading area or price Congestion pattern. All of the Congestion formations which we have studied in the preceding chapters—both Reversal and Consolidation types—are attended by a diminution in trading turnover. The more strictly defined sorts—the Triangles and Rectangles—show this characteristic most conspicuously. Moreover, activity in these patterns tends to be concentrated pretty much at or near the Top and Bottom edges, their Supply and Demand lines, while the area in between is a sort of "no-man's land." It is easy to see, therefore, why Gaps develop frequently within such areas. You will find many good examples of pattern Gaps in the charts.

Such pattern Gaps are usually closed within a few days, and, for obvious reasons, before the Congestion formation in which they have appeared is completed and prices break away from it. But not always. Sometimes a Gap will develop in the *last* traverse of prices across the pattern area just before a breakout, and in such cases, it is not closed for a long time, nor is there any reason why it should be.

The forecasting significance of Common or Pattern Gaps is practically nil. They have some use to the technician simply because they help him recognize an Area Pattern—that is, their appearance implies that a Congestion formation is in process of construction. If, for example, a stock moves up from 10 to 20, drops back to 17, and then returns to 20 making a Gap in the course of that rally, it is a fair assumption that further pattern development will take place between approximately 17 and 20. This is a convenient thing to know and may, on occasion, be turned to profit in short-term trading policy.

Pattern Gaps are more apt to develop in Consolidation than in Reversal formations. Thus, the appearance of many Gaps within an evolving Rectangle or Symmetrical Triangle reinforces the normal expectation that the pattern in question will turn out to be a Consolidation rather than a Reversal area.

BREAKAWAY GAPS

The Breakaway type of Gap also appears in connection with a price Congestion formation, but it develops at the *completion* of the formation in the move which breaks prices away. Any breakout through a *horizontal* pattern boundary, such as the Top of an Ascending Triangle, is likely to be attended by a Gap. In fact, it is safe to say that most of them are. And, if we consider what goes on in the market to create a flat-topped price formation, it is easy to see why Breakaway Gaps should be expected. An Ascending Triangle, for example, is produced by persistent demand for a stock meeting a large supply of it for sale at a fixed price. Suppose that supply is being distributed at 40. Other holders of the stock who may have intended originally to liquidate at 40 1/2 or 41 see quotations come up to 40 time after time, stop there and turn back. They tend, in consequence, either to join the crowd selling at 40, or else to figure that, once through 40, prices will go much higher; they may either lower or raise their selling price. The result is a "vacuum" on the books, a dearth of offerings in the price range immediately above the pattern. Hence, when the supply at 40 in our Ascending Triangle example is finally all absorbed, the next buyer of the stock finds none offered at 40 1/8 or 40 1/4; he has to bid up a point or more to get his shares, thus creating a Breakaway Gap.

CHART N

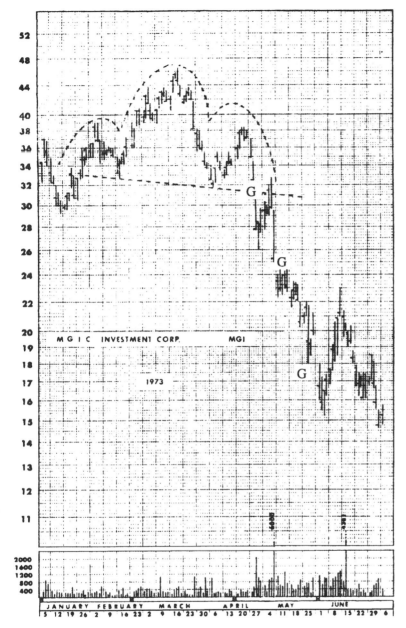

MGIC INVESTMENT—*This is a Head-and-Shoulders Top—actually, not the Top of the entire Major Upmove, which was reached in January, 1973, at approximately 100; nor the Top of the first rally, which occurred in mid-year of 1973 at around 80; but actually the peak of another secondary recovery in early 1974. Here, the price action traces the Head-and-Shoulders*

CHART N
(Continued)

MGIC INVESTMENT (Continued)—*very clearly, breaking away on the Downside with an Open Gap. Notice that even after the violation of the 22 level, and of the Head-and-Shoulders pattern, itself, the stock did make another attempt to come back, reaching a point somewhat above 32 before starting the next Downside plunge. Ordinarily, a pattern of this type will show heavier volume of trading on the left Shoulder, moderate volume on the Head, and only slight volume on the right Shoulder. However, the picture is plain enough, and, after the break on April 25, it spells trouble loud and clear. Within ten weeks, MGI was down to less than a third of what it had commanded at the March peak.*

CONTINUATION OR RUNAWAY GAPS

Less frequent in their appearance than either of the two forms we have discussed above, Gaps of the Continuation or Runaway type are of far greater technical significance because they afford a rough indication of the probable extent of the move in which they occur. For that reason, they have sometimes been called "Measuring" Gaps.

Both the Common or Pattern Gap and the Breakaway Gap develop in association with price formations of the area or Congestion type, the former within the formation and the latter as prices move out of it. The Runaway Gap, on the other hand, as well as the Exhaustion Gap, which we will take up later, are not associated with Area Patterns, but occur in the course of rapid, straight-line advances or declines.

When a dynamic move starts from an area of accumulation, the Upward Trend of prices will often seem to gather "steam," to accelerate for a few days, perhaps a week or more, and then begin to lose momentum as Supply increases when the very extent of the advance invites more and more profit taking. Trading volume jumps to a peak on the initial breakout, tapers off somewhat in the middle of the advance, and then leaps up again to a terrific turnover as the move is finally halted. In such moves—and in rapid declines of corresponding character—a wide Gap is quite likely to appear at the time when the Runaway is at its height, when quotations are moving most rapidly and easily with region to the volume of transactions. That period comes normally at just about the halfway point between the breakout which inaugurated the move and the Reversal day or Congestion Pattern which calls an end to it.

CHART O

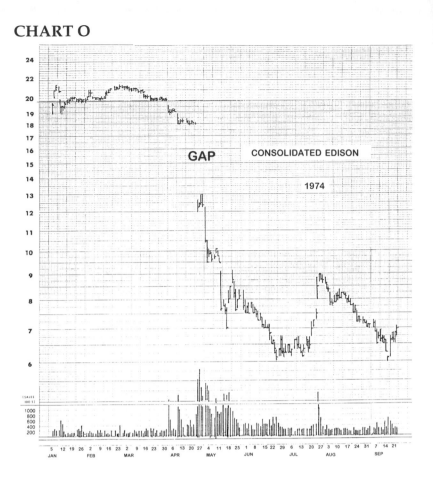

GAP CONSOLIDATED EDISON

1974

CONSOLIDATED EDISON—*If we take the history from early 1965, when it reached its all-time high of 49 1/4, we find that like almost all of the other Electric Utilities, ED had declined more than 50% by 1973. And, like most other Utilities, the dividends were steady, the earnings good. But, at 18, the stock did not look healthy as you can see. And then on Tuesday, April 23, the Bottom fell out completely, and, within four weeks, it was down to 7, later to 6. The stock was not showing strength at any point in 1974. It did not look like "a bargain" at 18. And it most certainly did not look like a bargain at any time after the great Downside Gap. ED is unusual only in that the breakdown was so spectacular. Actually, other stocks in the group have also looked unattractive to buy or sell. And, rather than considering these as "bargains," we would be asking why, if they are so good, should they be passed over by the important institutions in Wall Street? It would take some solid evidence of assertive, eager buying to make these Utilities look good. In a situation like this, it would seem best to stay out or sell short.*

Analyzing Bar Charts for Profit

EXHAUSTION GAPS

The Breakout Gap signals the start of a move; the Runaway Gap marks its rapid Continuation at or near its halfway point; the Exhaustion Gap comes at the end. The first two of these are easily distinguished as to type by their location with respect to the preceding price pattern, but the last is not always immediately distinguishable form the second.

Exhaustion Gaps, like Runaway Gaps, are associated with rapid, extensive advances or declines. We have described the Runaway type as the sort that occurs in the midst of a move, that accelerates to high velocity, then slows down again and finally stops as increasing Resistance overcomes its momentum.

THE ISLAND REVERSAL

The Island pattern is not common and it is not, in itself, of major significance, in the sense of denoting a long-term Top or Bottom, but it does, as a rule, send prices back for a complete retracement of the Minor move which preceded it.

An Island Reversal might be described as a compact trading range separated from the move which led to it (and which was usually fast) by an Exhaustion Gap, and from the move in the opposite direction which follows it (and which is also equally fast, as a rule) by a Breakaway Gap. The trading range may consist of only a single day, in which event, it normally develops as a One-Day Reversal, or it may be made up of from several days to a week or so of Minor fluctuations within a compact price zone. It is characterized, as might be expected, by relatively high volume. The Gaps at either end occur at approximately the same price level (they should overlap to some extent) so that the whole area stands out as an Island on the chart, isolated by the Gaps from the rest of the price path.

We have said that an Island does not of itself appear as a Major Reversal formation, but Islands frequently develop within the larger patterns at turning points of Primary or important Intermediate consequence, as, for example, in the Head of a dynamic Head-and-Shoulders Top. By the same token, they appear occasionally at the extremes of the Minor swings which compose a Triangle or a Rectangle (in which event, of course, the Gaps that set them off are really better classified as Common or Pattern Gaps).

The reasons why Islands can and do develop—in other words, why Gaps can and do repeat at the same price level—will be more apparent when we take up the general subject of Support and Resistance *(See Chapter 2).* Suffice it to repeat at this point, that prices can move most rapidly and easily, either up or down, through a range where little or no stock changed hands in the past, where, in other words, previous owners have no "vested interest."

Sometimes, the second Gap—the Breakaway that completes the Island—is closed a few days later by a quick pullback or reaction. More often it is not. Rarely, the first Gap—the Exhaustion Gap that starts the Island—is covered in a few days before the second Gap appears, in which even the Island Congestion takes on a sort of V-shape (if it is a Top) and there is no clear "open water" across the chart horizontally between the Island and the Trends preceding and following it. In any of these variations, however, the interpretation remains the same: the preceding Minor move should be practically retraced.

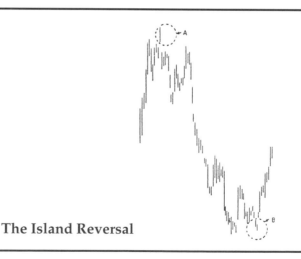

The Island Reversal

Analyzing Bar Charts for Profit

Chapter 7:
The Magee Method

John Magee's method of portfolio strategy for technical investing is diversification (we now call it asset allocation) by industry, geographic diversification, diversification by type of investment, and leverage. And a systematic strategy for minimizing losses and maximizing gains known as the trailing stop method of Trend following. For purposes of this discussion, however, we are only referring to the common stock position of one's portfolio. Protective stops are used for both long and short positions.

After a purchase has been made, a price is selected below which the stock will be sold at the market. This price is defined as the protective limit. It fixes (with rare exceptions) in advance how much we are willing to lose on a position. As a position moves higher, the limit is advanced. As long as a Trend "goes our way," we hold the stock and advance the limit. As soon as the Trend is broken, and the protective limit violated, we sell at the market.

PORTFOLIO STRATEGIES:
LIQUIDITY, INDUSTRY SELECTION, AND
NUMBER OF POSITIONS

How many stock positions should an investor own at one time? Which stocks should be included once the "ideal" number of positions has been determined? The answers to these seemingly straightforward questions are, in fact, quite complex because portfolio strategy depends in part on the needs and characteristics of each individual investor. The range of possible outcomes is extremely wide.

Perhaps, the most common mistake we have observed is that of the investor who buys small positions in so many stocks that he or she has trouble following them all. Moreover, each position tends to be such a small part of the whole that even a good job of managing a holding has little impact on one's total holdings.

The opposite extreme—that of "putting all one's eggs in one basket and then watching the basket closely"—carries the obvious risk that a single "bad" investment could wipe out a significant portion of one's assets.

Our experience suggests that portfolio diversification and managerial efficiency combine usefully when the number of positions varies from two to ten and funds available for investment vary from $10,000 to $200,000. For example, if an investor has $10,000 to invest initially, we would recommend the selection of two positions of $15,000 and $5,000 each. A $100,000 investor might begin with six or seven positions of $15,000 each. While at $200,000, approximately ten positions averaging $20,000 each would be appropriate. The benefits of diversification decline sharply as the number of positions held rises above ten; so for even a $1,000,000 account, we would recommend holding no more than ten to twelve positions.

Additional diversification criteria which we have found useful include *industry* and *liquidity*. For a theoretical $120,000 portfolio of eight $15,000 positions, we certainly would not want all eight positions to be in steel, or oil, or electronics, or any other *single* industry. So, we suggest a policy of individual stock selection which provides *industry* diversification. For our theoretical $120,000 portfolio, a "concentration limitation" of two holdings in any one industry (25% of total portfolio) is desirable, with one position per industry being ideal.

To the extent that one's stock positions become sizable (1,000 shares and up of a stock), we add "liquidity." As a stock position totals 100 shares or even a few hundred shares of a nationally listed company, a high degree of liquidity can be assumed. But when it is time to head for the exits with larger positions, one's ability to sell and move quickly may be sharply reduced in many of the "thinner," less actively traded stocks which may be found on the exchanges. Our rule is that no more than half the issues in any individual industry should be illiquid.

It may be difficult to think in terms of stocks to buy when the market is experiencing record days up or down, but in fact, this is the appropriate time. We recommend that you start putting together the stocks, and industry groups that you would like to participate in at the time when you feel a commitment could be profitable.

Chapter 8:
Selected Market Letters of John Magee (1982–1988)

This chapter is a collection of one-page editorials written week by week over a 6-year period for our Stock Advisory Service. These editorials were selected for their timelessness and educational value. If you look at the editorial entitled, "Currency Swings," you will find that history is repeating itself. We feel that these editorials are much better than many books we have read on the subject. We hope that you enjoy and learn as much as we have from them.

LONG-TERM CHART, YOUR LONG-TERM FRIEND

Although we do not comment on the likely direction of the popular market indices, choosing instead to concentrate on individual issues, the lengthy slump in the market as measured by these averages over the past nine months highlights the across-the-board weakness now prevalent. It also accounts for the widespread pessimism of investors, and the rise of the doom-and-gloom advisors.

Technical traders, however, should not be swayed by the swirl of poor economic factors giving rise to much of the current Bearish psychology. The charts should remain your guide, and the most important type of chart during periods of excessive pessimism or optimism are long-term. There is an understandable tendency for traders to use only daily charts for buy or sell signals. But as Magee and Edwards noted in *Technical Analysis of Stock Trends*: "Long-term or Major charts...are used chiefly for determining *important Support and Resistance* levels and marking long-term Trends." The *key* words are Support and Resistance levels. The Major Reversal or Continuation patterns found in daily charts will, of course, occur in weekly or monthly charts with "identical significance" as in daily charts. Volume may not be as useful since "climatic activity may occur on one day of a week and the other days run dull, which would not show at all in the week's total figure; but volume is less critical (than for daily charts) and may almost be disregarded."

Long-term charts—and we generally prefer monthly charts for a longer view—are important tools no matter what market conditions exist. That is why we add the small insert of monthly ranges on each of our illustrated issues. But the long-term picture is particularly important during hyper-extension periods in the stock market. Stocks always stop their directional movement somewhere, and more often than not, they will stop at an old Support or Resistance level.

For that reason, Major Support and Resistance levels are particularly significant during periods when markets appear to be overreaching themselves in one direction or the other. By carefully looking through his or her long-term charts, a technician can pinpoint areas where it is clear that significant Support (Resistance) will most likely be encountered to stop the current decline (advance)—at least temporarily—and from which a rally (reaction) can be expected to start.

The Mobil chart is a good illustration of the type of Support/Resistance points we look for during unusual weakness (strength). MOB established a high of 17 in 1969; dropped to Support at 9 in 1970; rose to 15 in 1971 (note the 1971 floor was the 1965-66 high); rallied to 19 in 1973; collapsed in 1974; rebounded to the 1969 high; pulled back to the 1970-71 highs; then rallied to its 1980 high where, a second test late in the year, formed a Double Top that sent MOB down throughout 1981. The key Support area on the way back down is the 1971 high to the 1973 high (14-19). Should MOB drop to that level, it would signal to our technical staff that an immediate buy recommendation was in order, or a close watch should be placed on the daily chart. It does take some additional time to work up and use long-term charts, but knowing where you are in a rapidly rising or declining market more than offsets the extra work.

FIGURE 1

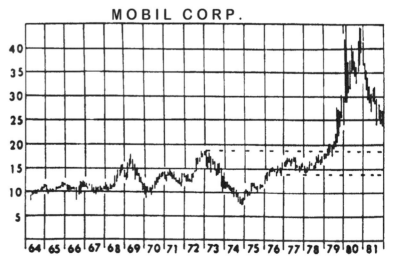

MOBIL CORP.

Analyzing Bar Charts for Profit

THE SHAPES BEHIND THE SHADOWS

One of the most baffling things in this business, where baffling things happen all the time, is the situation where somebody comes in and looks at the vast files of charts, scratches his head and remarks, "I just don't see how you can tell what's going to happen in the *future* from these chart records of market action."

We have to sit down and patiently explain that (a) we *can't* tell exactly what's going to happen in the future any more than anybody else can, and (b) the only way anybody can make intelligent plans about the future is from past experience and records and what would seem most likely to follow as a consequence. This is what weather forecasters and insurance underwriters do. And it is what engineers and doctors do. And it is about what everybody does, whether or not they actually make a chart of it.

It seems hard for the person who is neither an engineer nor trained in the mathematics of predictive methods to understand that a chart or other statistical record is neither an infallible guide to what will happen next; nor is it totally valueless in estimating the chances. Thus, the records and tables cannot absolutely assure us that tomorrow, May 23, we will not have a record temperature of 90°. These things do happen once in a while. But the past records suggest, even to a person who has never lived in these climes at all, that the odds in favor of a 90° day in May here are very slim.

So, we have to hammer on the desk and raise our voices to protest that no, we do *not* believe that any chart or diagram, index, average, or indicator can provide absolute promises about the future; not in this changing and uncertain world. And then we have to come right out and make our point; which is that the charts are not meaningless but are *charged* with meaning. And that they do frequently point toward "probable" (or "expected," or "hoped-for," or "feared") events in the future. And that for all their shortcomings and lack of absolute guarantees, we have found them at least as good, and probably better, in our experience, than any other way of evaluating a situation and its "most likely" future course.

It has seemed that the charts for a good many years have been saying, "Some very well-informed people with substantial financial clout have felt that the Steel stocks were not going to be doing as well as some others." Likewise, the Chemicals. And for the last eight years "something" (and it is *not* necessary to know *what*, though it would not be hard to name several reasons) has thrown the Office Equipment stocks into a sideways movement in spite of steadily rising earnings and dividends. The warning signs in the Oil stocks flashed on in early 1981 and remain on in many cases. The problems of high interest rates lit up the danger signals two years ago for Savings and Loan issues. Right now, we have an interesting situation in the Airlines; with some Airline stocks looking better than they have for a long time, and others still looking extremely weak. Is there any connection between these confusing Trends in the Airlines and the arbitrary and capricious shifting from regulation to deregulation (and possibly back again) by Federal agencies?

Charts cannot surely read the future. But they can surely indicate the *probabilities* of certain things happening, as seen by the sharpest and best-informed observers and reflected in stock prices and volume.

JUST ONE MORE TIME...*

A week or so ago, we tuned in to our favorite TV thrillers "Wall Street Week." After learning that the elves were unanimously Bullish and listening to the regular panel members opine that the market would go up if it didn't go down, we settled back to enjoy the invited guest—a market forecaster of great repute. And when Louis Rukeyser finally popped *the* question, "Do you think the market has seen its low?", we leaned forward eagerly to catch the cautious reply. "I think the market will have *one more downswing* before really taking off."

We've heard that before, more times than we care to remember. Just last September, when the prime rate reached 20 1/2%, the newspapers were full of "experts who expected just one more notch on the upside" before interest rates hit their peak. How many investors missed the ensuing rally in interest rate futures because they were waiting for just one more increase in the prime rate which now stands at 16%?

Whenever we hear such a prediction, we are immediately skeptical. It is too easy and too cautious an answer; and too likely to result in lost opportunity for the investor. What if there is no downswing? When does an investor conclude he was wrong and how long does he wait to enter the market? How much has the poor forecast cost him?

Part of the problem in trying to call Major market Tops and Bottoms to forecast the next Major move, is human nature itself. It seems cautious and reasonable to aver that although stock prices are depressed and near historic lows, even lower prices may occur before recovery sets in. Put another way, it is typical human behavior to project into the future that which

---

*   *Adapted from* Page One, *May 17, 1980, which was written at DJIA 826 just before the 175-point May/November DJIA rally.*

occurred in the immediate past. If the market falls this week as it has for several preceding weeks, one is likely to expect it to fall again the coming week.

True, there well may be "one more downswing" in the market. If it does occur and is *severe*, we will be ready with our protective limits and an occasional short recommendation. If a *moderate* downswing occurs, the majority of our long positions will probably test their limits before moving ahead. But we have already been paid well for our willingness to enter the market while investors expecting "another sell-off" stand on the sidelines. Promising advances are underway in AVX Corporation, American Sterilizer, Anheuser Busch, ARKLA, Atlantic Richfield, Cities Service, Ford Motor, General Foods, Johnson & Johnson, Medtronic, and NLT, to mention only a few.

And what if there is not another downswing? We will be well positioned to participate fully in any upswing *whenever it starts and as far as it goes*.

MANAGING MONEY

Let this be very specific. We are thinking of a particular man whom we know. His name is not Kenneth Hudson; but he is a very real person.

Ken has been highly successful and has a fine business reputation. The value of his securities at the time we first talked with him amounted to something over $300,000, a loss of about $100,000 from cost. At that time he appeared very worried, quite unhappy. If he is still holding the stocks he held then, he is considerably more worried and considerably more unhappy today.

There can be no question as to Ken's competence in his chosen field. For many years he ran a difficult family business very profitably. When it came time to sell, he negotiated an excellent transaction, divided proceeds with several family members, and started another successful business. He is regarded as a man of superior abilities, high intelligence, and great determination.

However, a single look at his portfolio, or an hour of conversation with Ken, and one realizes that he is absolutely ignorant of the nature of his securities, has had no training or preparation in this area, has no feeling of self-assurance or confidence, and suffers a great deal of anxiety.

Just for openers, he owns *41 different stocks and bonds.* Now there is such a thing as over-concentrating in a single stock, and there is a good deal to be said for having some diversification. But to follow the financial developments of 41 stocks and bonds at once is certainly beyond the abilities of anyone who is also working at a breakneck pace in his business or profession.

But there was more evidence of Ken's confusion. Within the common stock section of the portfolio, more than 50% of the holdings were in one industry And the holdings were unbalanced, ranging from as high as $30,000 in one issue to $3,000 in others.

Also the portfolio included, not a harmonious, but seemingly a random selection of ultra-conservative stocks, "Go-Go" issues, more or less standard securities of average habits, Over-the-Counter items, and some esoteric stocks, apparently in companies in which Ken had friends, relatives, or other close "inside connections or information."

All of this made it very clear why Ken looked so worried and so unhappy. The investment program upon which his retirement would depend was a mess. And this he probably knew. But he did not know what to do about it. Here he was: a brilliant and "successful" man with a considerable fortune. But in all the long years of his education, in courses which touched on economics, civics, and even finance, he had not had any definite instruction about stocks, bonds, the financial markets, and how they operate. And, like many others with a hard-working schedule and family responsibilities, he did not have the time nor the energy to start the education he had never received.

There is a "gap" and a lack of relevance in the highly specialized education which prepares so many people so well for "making a living" as doctors, lawyers, engineers, or business executives, but prepares them not at all to protect and to manage effectively the fruits of their life's work.

BUYING PANIC (AND WHAT IT MEANS)

Two records were set on Wall Street this week. Both may endure for quite some time. On Tuesday, the Dow Jones Industrial Average rose 38.81 points on near-record trading of 92,860,000 shares, the largest single-day advance in history. On Wednesday, an astounding total of 132.7 million shares traded hands, easily passing the 100-million-share milestone, as the DJIA retreated 1.81 points.

Tuesday's advance—a classical "buying panic"—was front-page news across the country. Economists and business experts were called upon to comment on the *reasons* for the upsurge. The consensus was that revised, more optimistic interest rate forecasts by two noted bond market experts had set the rally off. Other observers suggested that improving fundamental Trends had been underway in the capital markets for some time, and that Wall Street (as well as the two "experts") had simply become aware of that fact.

We have never cared much for analyzing the reasons behind this or that stock market move. A change in direction in Wall Street may be due to fundamental changes in the business environment, or to purely psychological causes. There may be one reason, or many reasons, for a *specific* move at a *given* time. We prefer to concentrate, instead, on analyzing the technical behavior of individual stocks monitored weekly by our staff and selecting those most attractive for purchase or short sale in accordance with the current position of the Magee Evaluative Index.

What can we say at this time about this most extraordinary stock market behavior? Did Tuesday's cathartic 38.81-point DJIA advance constitute a Major Reversal in the direction of the stock market? A review of *individual stock patterns* suggests that the answer to this question is "no, almost certainly not." Numerous stocks, we would say almost the majority, rallied from within a point or less of their recent, intermediate-term Downtrending lows. We are unaware of any technical case for describing such behavior as Bottom-like. The proportion of stocks rated Strong currently stands at a relatively low 18%. Single-day high-volume spikes *alone* do not constitute Reversal patterns. In fact, the number of stocks which have formed valid, recognizable three-week to three-month (or longer) patterns which we customarily associate with Reversals remains extremely low.

What has happened, then, and what does it mean? First, Wall Street has been treated to a rally, the best one-day rally ever. Importantly, the brokerage industry functioned extremely well, handling the record-setting activity in an orderly, confidence-building way. Secondly, the lift-off in many stocks was great enough to constitute an important potential *first leg* of the Bottom-forming process in many individual stocks. What is required individually (and collectively for the market as a whole) is a lower volume pullback to Support, and a high-volume subsequent upmove *through* the interim highs set on Tuesday. Then (and only then) can we talk about a meaningful *technical* Bottom being in place.

Perhaps Tuesday's one-day rally is a straw in the wind. Certainly, the MEI is in clear-cut Bullish territory. And certainly, the interest rate climate for equities has improved dramatically recently (see "Change in the Wind?," *Page One*, August 7, 1982). If so, the number of Strong-rated issues should begin to increase notably in the weeks and months ahead; profit opportunities among the numerous stocks off fifty percent or more from their highs will abound. In the meantime, *some* individual stocks continue to swim against the tide with classically developed Bottoming patterns already in place. We continue to advocate the careful accumulation of these stocks with purchases spaced over time and protective limits honored if necessary. Experience has shown that these "early bloomers" are often the best gainers following sustained MEI readings within the Bullish Quartile.

Analyzing Bar Charts for Profit

DANGEROUS SPIKES

During the recent stock market explosion, a common Bottoming pattern has occurred which is anything but common, technically. Specifically, many stocks—just after piercing Support and establishing a *new trading low*—have reversed direction dramatically to establish new interim trading highs, breaking through one or more levels of Resistance in the process.

The three charts shown are particularly dramatic examples of this unusual technical behavior. In the case of Alleghany Corporation, a new trading low of 35 5/8 was reached early last month easily exceeding previous important lows of 37 1/4 (July, 1982) and 41 1/8 (March, 1982), and confirming the Downtrend then in force. Within three weeks, however, Y had soared to 43, decisively penetrating July Resistance at 41 7/8. The moves in American Express (35 to 46) and Western Union (25 to 34) showed similar disregard for classic Bottoming behavior as well as for previous Resistance levels.

These unique spike Reversals from new lows to new highs show many similarities with the broadening, or "Megaphone" patterns usually associated with Major Tops (see Edwards and Magee, *Technical Analysis of Stock Trends*). Because successively lower lows are interspersed with progressively higher highs, these patterns inherently reflect price instability and increasing volatility. Stated another way, *it is impossible to state technically whether such an issue is in a Downtrend or an Uptrend.*

Despite the seeming attractiveness of such turn-on-a-dime stocks, we have avoided recommending these issues in recent weeks. Instead, more classic Trendline Reversals combined with traditional Bottom formations have been favored. If we did find ourselves owning these spiking issues, we would be inclined to sell or sell short against the box at least half the position. Or, as an alternative, to write covered calls at a strike price near or slightly below the current market price.

To the extent that these dramatic spike rallies reflect the enthusiastic reaction of investors to the recent sharp decline in interest rates, they may be regarded as a Bullish signal of better times ahead. In selecting which stocks to buy now, however, we continue to favor those with the Reversal patterns typically associated with the technical Bottoming process.

FIGURE 2

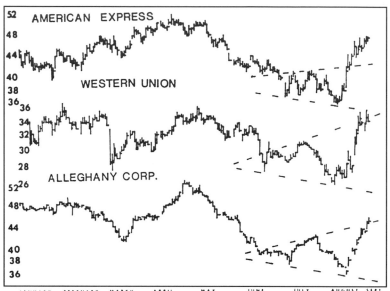

Analyzing Bar Charts for Profit

REFLECTIONS

This week we were both pleased and honored to receive a copy of a small booklet entitled "The Stock Market Innovators Survey." We were pleased because the book contained a compilation of the investment strategies of twelve professionals "whose consistent success" supports the premise that "there are investment strategies and stock picking techniques which, albeit imperfect, vastly improve our ability to profit from buying and selling common stocks"; and honored, because our technical work at John Magee Inc. is the subject of one of the book's chapters. We particularly enjoyed reading the comments (reprinted here with the permission of the publisher) of William LeFevre, Investment Strategist, Purcell Graham & Company; Inc., regarding the inability of many investors to "recognize" a Bull Market—particularly in the *early* stages—when one is upon them:

> "The consensus opinion is always late to recognize the existence of a new Bull Market. In most cases, Bull Markets are not widely acknowledged until one-third of the move has already occurred. This is infinitely understandable considering the emotional factors involved in investing in stocks, and the enormous influence of institutional investors in today's market. It takes time and some palpable proof of better times ahead before the fear created by a previous slide gives way to greed as the dominant emotion in the market. Recently burned, currently cautious. This is true of the institutions as well as the man on the street. Also, because of the sheer size of institutional investments—70% or more of the total volume on the NYSE—it is even more difficult for them to reverse gears. Consequently, the chart pattern of a new Bull Market disguises a good deal of its momentum. In the early stages of a Bull Market, a DOW or S&P chart displays a saw-tooth pattern. Advances are often interrupted by declines. It is essential to note,

however, that the market advances on increased volume, and declines during periods of relatively inactive trading. Each advance and each decline takes the market to a point higher than the previous advance peak or trough. What's happening is that institutions, which missed the initial moves, are simply waiting for a correction before increasing their commitments. When they do jump in, volume spikes and the market moves higher. So, the moral of the story is that consensus opinion does not recognize a new Bull Market until its horns protrude far enough to 'needle' the Bears into buying stocks."

We are reminded of the disbelievers who have recently been predicting a "100- to 150-point decline" in the DJIA, failing to acknowledge the significance of the recent move by the DJIA to new all-time highs after having been turned back at Dow 1000 or thereabouts for nearly *seventeen years*.

We have made the point often recently, and we make it again; do not let the cries of these stock market Cassandras, or the buildup of large profits in your investments, make you so nervous that you sell out otherwise perfectly healthy positions. Evaluate each stock on its individual merits. *Hold onto a position as long as it is technically strong*. When it turns weak, *sell it without fail*. Leave the forecasting of the market's twists and turns to those who have more elegant crystal balls, many of whom have yet to recognize this Bull Market. Perhaps another upleg (or two) will finally "needle" them aboard also.

March 12, 1983

WE FOLLOW THE TAPE NOT THE TUBE

We enjoy Liz and Jack and their "Eyewitness" local news; and Dan Rather for the national perspective. Also, you will find us watching "Meet the Press" (and even "Wall Street Week") on occasion.

So much for television news for a limited but rewarding yield of commentary, entertainment, and excitement.

But for the *facts* concerning the state of the nation, or the world, the economy, and the outlook for things to come, we'd lean more on the evaluations of those who are, as the saying goes, "putting their money where their mouth is." And their activities are made manifest in a narrow strip of electronics or printed characters which is ejected fitfully from a black box. *The Tape.* A probe into "their" activities.

"They" are largely anonymous; these thousands of investors, traders, institutional buyers, and the Gnomes of Zurich. "They" do not tell us "why" they are so anxious to acquire the Airlines or to unload the Oils. They just risk their personal or corporate fortunes. They literally stake their economic lives on their judgments. And it seems altogether unnecessary that we should know the "whys."

And for our money, we'd be more inclined to accept their judgments rather than the opinions of some rewrite man in the City Room or the emotionally charged editorial views of the various radio and TV commentators who would explain to us what the reported facts "really meant."

In other words, we like to get as close as possible to original sources and direct evidence, and to make *our own* interpretations in arriving at our evaluations, rather than accept the judgments of news media "interpreters."

On the whole, we feel the tape is a better criterion of truth than the tube or the news media for that matter.

Not that the tape or any other gauge is an infallible predictor of the future. It is necessary, always, to make judgments tentatively and to be ready to revise or completely reverse an opinion if changes occur in the underlying conditions.

But, check your own experience. Consider the pessimistic business reports last summer and through year-end as the stock market mounted its 300-point advance to historic new highs. Compare the outcome of your strategies which have been guided by the tape, as compared with your experiences when you have reacted to the news or the headlines or the well-meant words of wisdom offered by your next-door neighbors.

March 19, 1983

"SECOND PHASE" STOCKS:
SOME TECHNICAL OBSERVATIONS

Every stock must be analyzed for its unique, individual technical characteristics before an investment decision is made. From time to time, however, stocks separate themselves into one or more *groups*, analysis of which often proves helpful in the investment decision-making process.

In October, when we last commented on groupings of technical patterns, a dominant formation was *Accelerating Uptrend stocks*, i.e., stocks which were pulling rapidly away from their constant growth rate Trendlines. Such issues were described as "vulnerable to short-term Reversals which would return them, at the least, to their Intermediate Uptrend lines." Currently, two additional technical positions are appearing regularly among actively traded AMEX and NYSE-listed issues. We have commented on the first, the "Stairstep Uptrend," often in this service; the trailing stop method of protective limits is easily applied to the successive price and volume waves of the pattern, making it relatively easy to "manage" technically.

A second recurring pattern of significance is more complex. It extends over a longer period of time and consists of:

1. A **Major advance of 90% to 100%** (either steady or Accelerating Uptrend);

2. A **Consolidation-like** pattern which could have been either a Top or a Continuation pattern; and

3. A **subsequent high volume Upside Breakout**.

We have labeled such issues "Second Phase" stocks (analogous to the second phase of a Bull Market), referring to the likelihood that the area Breakout implies a new, probably substantial, advance in the price of the stock.

The chart of Motorola (recommended long, July 31, 1982) provides an excellent illustration. Between March and October, 1982, MOT rallied back to its 1981 high above 90 from a low of 49 1/4 (see Figure 3 below). Thereafter, from November to late December, MOT oscillated indecisively between 80 and the mid-90s before booming through to a new high on huge volume.

We conclude that MOT has entered a new (and important) "Second Phase" of advance. Other "Second Phase" stocks among our open positions are General Electric, International Flavors and Fragrances, National Medical Enterprises, Pitney Bowes, Pall Corporation and Santa Fe Industries. The emergence of these "Second Phase" uplegs is distinctly different from technical developments after rallies in the "stop-start" stock markets of the mid- to late 1970s and augurs well for the continuing health of the current Bull Market.

FIGURE 3

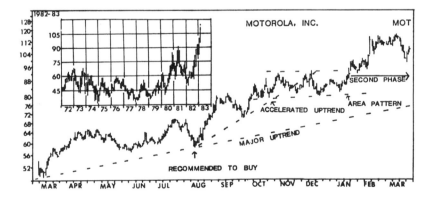

Analyzing Bar Charts for Profit

NEW ISSUES, HIGH TECHNOLOGY, WONDER STOCKS, AND THE LIKE

Recently, in one of our favorite daily financial publications, we read about "the return of the little guy" to the stock market. On the Front Page. There was the paving contractor from Chicago who dumped a considerable portion ($1,300) of his rainy day "nest egg" into 1000 shares of TechBomb (not its real name) at $1.25 per share. Before the day was over, his mother had invested $700 in the company and his younger brother $1,300. "It's like going to Las Vegas," he was quoted as saying. "Don't sit around worrying about it. Just do it."

The article went on to mention several other new issues, high technology, and wonder stocks which have captivated the public's imagination recently, often doubling or tripling in a short period of time. This is not to say that all new issues or concept stocks are hot air, or close to it, or even that most of them are. But the enthusiasm generated by the current Bull Market, as with every Bull Market, is undoubtedly producing excesses particularly dangerous to the new or uninformed investor.

It all reminds us of a piece we wrote a year or so ago entitled "Hole-In-One." We noted at the time:

> "No sane golfer would announce his or her intention
> of making a hole-in-one, this afternoon, on the next
> hole..." Although most people, consciously or uncon-
> sciously, realize that a hole-in-one is a combination
> of good golf and good luck, it is strange how many
> people go out to play a much tougher game than golf
> for the first time in their lives, set their ball up on the
> tee, whack it down the fairway or into the woods,
> and then wonder why they didn't make a hole-in-
> one. They go into the stock market on a gamble, tip,
> or rumor, staking savings they cannot afford to lose

on the most speculative stocks, without diversification or predetermined loss limits.

"Champion golfers do not depend on holes-in-one or 'all or nothing' drives. Successful investors do not depend on hot tips and new issues to convert excessively margined, speculative positions to 'once in a lifetime' profits. Successful people depend on methods which can advance their interests in good times... and also protect their interests in hard times. Like bridge players making the most of the cards they hold, good or bad."

What really amazes us is that *many of these new investors are buying stocks for which no previous price or volume data exist.* Do they not know that when a company strikes a bargain to go public it invariably tries to obtain the best possible price for its shares? Only occasionally, *very* rarely, do stocks—especially new issues—double or triple in a matter of weeks or months. In times such as these, the established Edwards and Magee philosophy of Trend following utilizing protective limits is of particular importance. Not flashy, perhaps, but rational, systematic, and time-tested over years of practical application.

Incidentally, the shares of TechBomb were last quoted at $1.12.

BEYOND THE LIMITS

Aside from wanting to know what's hot, or how far the DJIA will go up (or down), the most frequently asked questions we receive have to do with protective stop limits.

Most of the inquiries on the subject ask about a particular limit for a particular stock. Others, however, want a specific formula for limit placement. And a few suggest that we have substantially deviated from John Magee's methodology.

It is true that there has been a change in our method of setting limits over the past few years. John Magee wrote about using a formula based on a limit 5% under the last minor low, adjusted for volatility and stock price level (higher-priced issues make smaller percentage moves than lower-priced ones). The crux of this formula was a Sensitivity Index; but it did not prove to be particularly successful over the years and ultimately was discarded by the current staff.

However, as Mr. Magee wrote, "There is no perfect and absolutely satisfactory rule." We agree that a hard and fast formula is not practical. In general, our guideline for establishing protective stop limits is as follows. The *initial* or *opening limit* for a stock is placed at a point where important Support is evident (under a trading range or Channel, under a Major low, etc.). Most often, this will be a relatively wide limit reflecting several substantial Support zones which have evolved in the basing pattern preceding our recommendation. An important objective of these initially wide opening limits is to provide every opportunity for a new recommendation to achieve its potential.

As a stock progresses in our favor, limits are advanced more aggressively. We specifically watch Trendlines, Minor lows, Support-Resistance points and Gaps. Especially important is the point which, if violated on a closing basis, indicates a change in the Major Trend. For those who wish to fine tune the limit-setting process to include intra-weekly limit adjustments, we refer you to the section on progressive stop orders in *Technical Analysis of Stock Trends*, Edwards and Magee).

We also use, on occasion, arbitrary "buy or sell at the market" exit orders. In particularly fast-moving situations (often after a merger announcement) , where straight line advances (or declines) make the placement of *protective stop order* limit orders particularly difficult or dangerous, this type of exit is advisable.

While these general principles apply to perhaps 90% of protective limit-setting situations, there will always be that difficult 10% of the time when "the rules do not seem to apply." Consultation with our staff is recommended in such cases. In addition, subscribers may wish to trade against their open positions (i.e., sell part of a position on extraordinary strength, buy back on the pullback; or sell and repurchase covered calls), all within a period of time when no limit violation has taken place.

"It is understood, of course, that protective stops under long stocks are never moved down, nor are protective stops over shorts ever moved up." While we have modified our method of setting limits over the years, this fundamental principle of protective limits remains inviolate.

Analyzing Bar Charts for Profit

EVEN A STOPPED CLOCK IS RIGHT TWICE A DAY

We know of a widely followed investment advisor who successfully predicted the Bear Market which ended last summer. Correct as to timing and direction, his predictions were unfulfilled in one area. He expected a third (and final) leg of decline, from 750 to perhaps 550 on the DJIA. When the market turned up in August, rising from under 800 to over 1200 in a matter of months, our friend (and his clients) were still short stocks, and long cash. He had missed the upmove entirely. Currently this counselor has advised his clients that "1983 is a Major bubble that will translate into a Major adjustment which historians will later call a crash."

Investors (and investment advisors) are often strongly opinionated. Once a decision has been made to buy (or sell) American Widget, the facts seem to fall into place. The market looks stronger (weaker), earnings are headed up (down), dividends have just been increased (decreased), short interest is at a new high (low)...the list goes on and on.

Similarly, long lists of "reasons" are given by experts explaining why the market has been declining recently, or why it will advance shortly: Trends in business, money market conditions, political developments, long-term waves, and even the phase of the moon. There is no shortage of serious, well-meaning attempts to "explain" the stock market of the past, or to predict the stock market of the future.

This is not a frivolous exercise, by any means. But it is fraught with the danger that once we have bought or sold a stock, we will continue to marshall information in a manner which supports our original conclusion, rather than reflects what the market itself is telling us.

Where investors have trouble is in failing to recognize that all situations change and there is no perfect and complete way of knowing what changes and developments will occur. The trouble, a very big trouble, is that we learn from earliest childhood to make "positive" and "absolute" decisions, and to stick to them, to support them in every possible way. As though it would hurt us to revise an opinion. As though it would humiliate us to have to take a new look and correct our original observations or add something to them.

We are not alarmed or comforted by general stock market forecasts whatever the origin. The source of *profits* is the successful establishment (and closing out) of specific investment positions. We trust that our subscribers will remain alert for any signs of changing Trends in their individual holdings, and respond promptly and decisively when (and if) such changes are evident.

JUMPING THE GUN

On September 10, 1983, Mary Kay was recommended to "buy on stop" at 29. Attention was called to the "emerging" Inverse Head-and-Shoulders pattern. "The only element needed to confirm the turn would be a high-volume penetration (3%) of the Neckline," it was noted. In the weeks following our recommendation, after failing to activate our buy on stop, Mary Kay plunged to a new low of 15 7/8, more than 13 points below our buy on stop price.

Unfortunately, after such an occurrence, we almost invariably receive a phone call from a distraught, often relatively new subscriber and friend, who asks "what shall I do with my Mary Kay position—I have a terrible loss." Our reply just as invariably is "sell it out. Mary Kay looks terrible, technically."

Our new subscriber has committed one of the most common mistakes of technical analysis—"jumping the gun," we call it. It consists of *buying before a breakout.* The mistake is common in that almost every chartist at one time or another enters a pattern before it is completed; and understandable, because the rewards of early entry can be significant—often a price advantage of one to several points in the cost of a position.

The problem is, of course, that *a developing pattern is not actionable, technically, until it has been completed.* As an example, consider the potential Head-and-Shoulders formation of Mary Kay and the *completed* Head-and-Shoulders pattern of Wang Labs (recommended to buy at the market, September 17, 1983). While it was evident to our technical staff that MKY was well along the way in forming a classic Head-and-Shoulders pattern, the final Neckline penetration was clearly lacking at the time of recommendation.

In the case of Wang, a reasonably high-volume penetration of the Neckline on Friday, September 16 had completed the Head-and-Shoulders formation. Subsequent price activity confirmed the directional implications of the completed formation. And although Wang has retreated sharply over the past two weeks, the protective limit of 30 promises an acceptable loss in the range of 10% to 15% should Wang break down. In contrast, *when "developing" or "potential" Reversals break down, becoming Continuation patterns in the process, the move out of the pattern is often very sharp* (and therefore very costly to "early entrants").

We must admit to having had, initially, more than our share of doubt about the wisdom of ever "paying more for a stock than its current price." But over many years and stock market cycles, and countless thousands of charts, we have grown to appreciate the importance—even the essential nature—of this basic tenet of technical analysis. Paying the extra cost of having waited for a breakout (and formal pattern completion) is akin to paying an insurance premium for protection against catastrophe. Technically speaking, "jumping the gun" *invites* catastrophe.

FIGURE 4

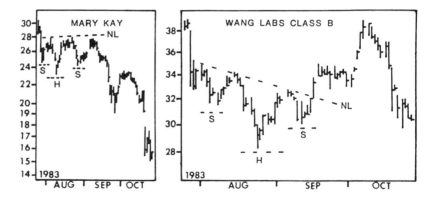

A PREVALENT PATTERN

Last week, on *Page One*, we reviewed the July/August Crash of Delta Airlines, and the subsequent development of a two-tier Rectangle Reversal pattern ("Now that looks like a Bottom"). This week, rather than analyze a single pattern as it relates to an individual stock, we consider a particular pattern which appears to be the prevalent technical pattern in the stock market at this time—the Double Bottom.

Figure 5 is a typical example of this pattern—Northwest Airlines. From its June, 1983 high of 55 1/2, NWA plunged to 36 by August 26. A One-Day Reversal selling climax established the base for Leg 1. The right side of the September 30 test of this level showed appropriate low volume to suggest a Double Bottom formation. Four weeks later, NWA escaped the pattern on the upside, confirming Reversal of the prevailing Downtrend.

A common characteristic of the many potential or actual Double Bottoms forming currently is low volume on the right side of Leg 2. While these patterns have evolved in as short a time as six weeks, and as long a period as seven months, three to six months is the usual case.

The recent development of numerous potential and actual Double Bottoms corresponds logically with the present low (Bullish) reading of the MEI Oscillator—an encouraging form of "double confirmation" regarding the current stock market outlook. Also of note, is that many of the stocks currently forming these patterns are doing so at prices sharply below recent high. The profit potential of new commitments is, therefore, substantial.

One word of caution: potential Support areas can turn into very Major Tops if a stock closes below its Support Neckline. (See Commodore Corporation recommended to sell short

October 15, 1983.) It is essential, therefore, to close out a position immediately in the event such a pattern does break down.

FIGURE 5

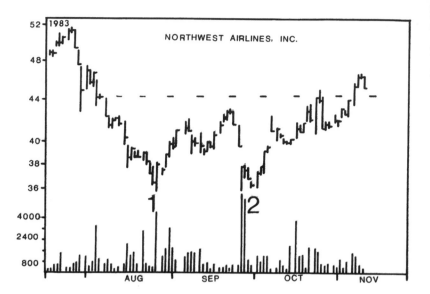

Analyzing Bar Charts for Profit

THE REASON(S) FOR THE MOVE

Rarely, if ever, do we feature the same chart in two consecutive editions of *Page One*. This week, however, the instant gratification from copper's breakaway explosion was simply too powerful to ignore. After leaping out of the *potential* Reversal pattern on a 100-point Gap on Monday, it advanced Wednesday to a high of 69.30 before retreating. For agile traders, the 300+ point, three-day move was tantamount to a 75% profit per fully margined copper contract. Impressive gains were also posted by copper-related stocks such as Newmont Mining and Phelps-Dodge, as well as by other metal issues caught up in the storm.

We have no idea as to the *reasons* behind Monday's sudden explosion in copper. And we were more than a bit surprised (and amused) to read that it was all due to last week's great London gold robbery!

> "The price of gold on international markets climbed $18 an ounce yesterday, to its highest level in more than a month, sparked by the weekend theft of three tons of bullion..."
> "Currency Markets", *The New York Times*, November, 29, 1983.

> "Copper on COMEX rose 135 to 125 points at the close in response to higher gold and silver prices".
> *The Journal of Commerce*, (November 30, 1983).

And there you have it. The surge in copper was due to the work of a gang of London gold thieves!

Our own thought processes admittedly being somewhat slow, we are skeptical of the "reasons" for the gold (and copper) advances as reported in our favorite newspapers. With just a slight stretch of the imagination we could envision a happy group of suddenly wealthy thieves sitting around a cauldron, melting down their $37 million in ill-gotten gold, *readying it for return to the marketplace.* The result in our mind—little or no effect on supply and demand.

Our founder, John Magee, summarized his views on the reasons for market moves most eloquently:

> "Every now and then some stock, a group of stocks, or the whole market, which has been lying dormant for weeks, suddenly takes off in a great explosion of activity.
>
> "Some people will say, 'Well, there must be a *reason* in back of this activity.'
>
> "It may be a good reason, it may be a bad reason, it may be a reason not directly related to the company, but perhaps to politics, international affairs, matters of control or merger of corporations, etc. There could be *two reasons, three, many reasons, all true.*
>
> "We prefer to study carefully *what* is going on in the market, to make our inferences and decisions on that and not to dig too deeply into the rich, confusing veins, arguments, and hypotheses."

We couldn't agree more.

FIGURE 6

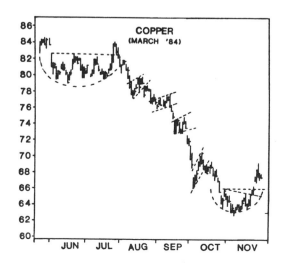

Analyzing Bar Charts for Profit

MEDIA WONDERS

We understand that Wednesday morning, on a popular "news" show, a widely-followed stock market advisor expressed his strong opinion to the effect that the market was headed lower, probably substantially so. This "expert" has reportedly had an excellent forecasting record in recent years, and the stock market responded with due respect. Prices opened lower with the tape several minutes behind. At the close, the Dow Jones Industrial Average was down 8.90 points to 1143.63, just a shade above its low for the year.

We're aware of some other interesting "calls" authoritatively reported by the media recently. Like the Thursday, February 16, 1984 headline in the *Wall Street Journal*: "Foreign Currencies Seen Opening Lower As Profits Are Taken." That was the day that the major currencies—the British Pound, the Swiss Franc, the German Mark, and the Japanese Yen, all opened sharply higher. In fact, the low prices set on that day haven't been seen since!

In similar vein, we were amused by a headline in the *New York Times* (February 13, 1984) which proclaimed: "Panic Cited by Traders In Stocks' 3-Week Fall." Rather self-evident, we thought, if not outright *definitional*. And in the same Business Section: "Interest Rates Appear Headed Up This Year," according to credit market specialists who are reversing their recent forecasts of easier rates. Worth a chuckle, at least, the prominence given the forecasts of these "experts."

For our own part, if there is anything which should be focused on at a time like this, it is *what the market is saying about a particular stock and what the price and Trend are.* The price is what one must pay for a stock if he or she wants it; and the price is all one gets if selling that stock; and we don't know that there is other information in the picture that would stand above these facts as they are stamped out on the tape.

So far as the "fundamental" approach versus "technical" analysis, if a stock is moving up, or down, or sideways, in our mind the present price probably reflects all the published statistics, all the earnings expectations, dividend projections, interest rates, tax prospects, overseas competition, leverage, as well as what a cousin of one of the directors told us in confidence at the club last night, off the record.

It seems to us that whenever the stock market is noteworthy enough to become "news," it is during a period of relative under- or over-valuation; both the euphoria of Bull Markets and the panic of declining markets make good news copy. It is precisely at such times, however, that we counsel avoidance of tips, news headlines—even the opinions of "experts" who were "right" last time. Concentrate instead on the price and volume behavior of individual stocks, on a case-by-case basis, in accordance with the Edwards and Magee method of technical analysis. No crystal ball is required!

DRIFTERS

In life, no one, we suppose, knowingly wants to be associated with "drifters." In the stock market, however, there is a time when "drifting" stocks are perfectly acceptable buy or sell candidates.

To put matters in perspective, the majority of stocks have been undergoing rolling readjustments after chalking up spectacular gains from their 1982 lows. IBM is an excellent example. From our 1982 entry point of 58, it soared to a high of 134 last October before being closed out several weeks later on a limit violation at 119. Thereafter, it continued to drift downward, but at a slower and slower rate of decline, until finally a series of stairstep upmoves reversed the Downtrend, validating Support at 107 in the process.

FIGURE 7

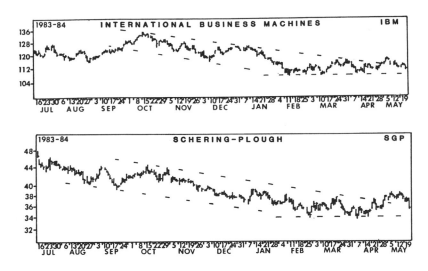

Schering-Plough Corporation, another recent recommendation exhibits similar "drifter" characteristics. From its mid-1983 high of 48, it Trended steadily downward to a low of 34 before establishing sufficient upward momentum to achieve a Reversal, and validate Support at 34.

This behavior by IBM and SGP is, to date, compatible with the general framework of a first reaction after a Major Bull move in each stock. Whether a second Major Bull Leg lies ahead for these issues will not be established finally until they top their previous peaks. And quite negative conclusions would be justified should either stock close below the recently established Support levels referred to above.

The "drifting" pattern, while not a typical Major Bottoming or Topping formation such as the Head-and-Shoulders, or Rectangle, is nevertheless highly useful during the first reaction after a Major up or down move. Akin to "Fan Lines," it signals the point at which forces in the direction of the Major Trend are reasserting themselves; and thereafter, provides highly relevant points for confirmation or non-confirmation.

BIG MONEY IN BRAIN SURGERY:
LEARN AT HOME THIS QUICK, EASY WAY

Some Wall Street wisdom is timeless. This commentary, written by John Magee on July 23, 1966, is as insightful today as it was eighteen years ago.

It always fazes us a little to realize how many people spend so much time, money, and effort, apparently in a quest to discover the "hidden secrets" of the stock market. Mr. Average Man who has a few thousand dollars to invest and who may have a very keen understanding of his own business or profession, so often comes to Wall Street with the bright hope that he is going to find the magic word, or the crystal ball, or the unfailing oracle; a hope, by the way, that is not likely to be realized.

He will keep trying *this* formula or *that* "system" in much the same spirit that one might go out in the woods on a misty morning and peek behind every big rock along the way in the expectation that sooner or later he might find a Leprechaun hiding there.

It is not that he is unwilling to put further effort, or to spend money and time in his search. It is that he is searching in the wrong places for something that doesn't actually exist as he imagines it.

So often he is seeking something that will provide a degree of certainty that nobody can expect in this world. He does not realize that the market evaluation is a thing in flux, a day-to-day balance of the prospects for this stock or that stock; and these prospects can be influenced by conditions that cannot be predicted with certainty, or in some situations cannot be predicted at all. Let a big contract be cancelled, let a new "pocket war" break out somewhere, let any new circumstance come into the economy or into the affairs of a single company, and the market will revalue the stock accordingly. No method, scheme, or plan that we know of can anticipate everything that may happen in the future. The most that one can hope to accomplish is to estimate the reasonably expectable consequences of a set of presently known conditions. There remains a big area of uncertainty; and an essential part of the investor's problem is to recognize this, accept it, and understand that a considerable part of his strategy must be to learn how to cope with conditions when they do not work out as he had anticipated, or when new conditions result in new Trends. He must learn not to make his original judgments "too absolute" and learn how to defend himself when they must be changed.

And, too, the new investor is often trying to reduce the market to a much-too-simple affair. He will cram his bookshelves and his desk with reports and data, stuff his head with figures, master a dozen rule-of-thumb "methods." He will have facts, sometimes too many *irrelevant* facts. And he may not realize that thousands of people are watching the market, studying it, analyzing it by various means, making their evaluations in their own ways; and some of these people have a great deal of insight plus a great deal of experience. They know what to do "if all goes well, according to rule," but they also know when "it is time to throw the book out the window" and improvise.

We believe that this ability to roll with the punch, to confront new or unexpected situations with courage and calmness, doesn't come from theory alone or facts alone, but from deep awareness of both the mechanics and the psychology involved; a knowledge that usually comes hard, and is learned mostly in the "School of Hard Knocks." Like brain surgery, it is a matter not to be acquired in a few easy lessons; but by actual experience and insight.

FORECASTING:
NO SUCH THING AS A SURE THING

Almost nightly we turn on the television (or call the weather number) to hear a rather pleasant fellow as he tells us about the low extending southward from Pennsylvania and extending as far west as the Mississippi; the Canadian cold front, now moving slowly Southeastward at a speed of about ten miles per hour; the relative humidity; present temperature at Logan Airport; and the small craft warnings from Block Island to Long Island Sound. Also, that the next two days will be marked by much colder air moving into the area, and chances of precipitation are three out of ten.

To a good many people, this is either (a) the gospel, or (b) the next best thing to it.

It is certainly not the gospel, however. There are competent men and women with long experience in the Weather Bureau, who are telling us what the *probabilities* seem to be at this time in the light of their knowledge and the data before them. They would be the first to tell you that they do not know *with certainty* what the weather will be on Sunday, because winds can shift and new factors can come into the picture. But, taking it on balance, the predictions do represent an informed and intelligent "estimate" of what is most likely to happen. And yet there are some people who feel personally injured when rain appears at the picnic instead of the "sunny and clear" which was predicted; and want to go down and take a swing at the poor, hard-working weatherman.

Sometimes a meteorological prediction is quite definite. The other night our friendly weatherman wrote on the board under chances of precipitation the figures 10/10, that is ten chances out of ten, or "certainty." Actually, we did get some rain. But if you had pinned him down on that 10/10 prediction, he would undoubtedly have conceded that a more realistic figure might have been 95/100 or 98/100; "close to" certainty, but not "absolute." There is always a certain element of doubt, calling for tentative judgment. It is good to know what seems most likely to happen; but always necessary to be prepared to revise a plan when and if data changes.

In stocks many investors are likely to accept the reports or data they may have as "final" and "absolute," the veritable "sure thing." But the stock that looked strong in August may run into trouble; a reduced dividend, a bad quarterly report, or whatever. And the very weak-looking stock may turn around and start up. Operating successfully in an environment of uncertainty, however, is not "just a matter of luck." It is possible to make reasonable and good recommendations and decisions so long as one realizes that stocks, like the weather, are continually changing and call for the ability of an investor to change his or her mind when conditions call for it. In fact, there is no such thing as a *sure* thing. Consistent success requires constant monitoring of a stock's Trend and the flexibility to recognize and take action if the Trend changes.

WHICH WAY THE MARKET: AND WHY

Everyone wants to know "which way the market will go." Trouble is, nobody *really* knows. Usually, there are numerous opinions as to the future course of stock prices, and just as numerous "theories" behind those opinions. From time to time, there is even a *consensus* most of the "experts" who have an opinion agree. When that does happen, however, often as not the exact *opposite* actually occurs.

Granted, forecasting the future of *anything* is difficult; in the stock market, particularly so. In fact, so complex are the workings of the stock market that few "experts" can even agree on the reasons for market movements which have *already* occurred. Our favorite source of entertainment on this score is the stock market column which appears daily in just about every newspaper. Some recent examples:

On September 27, in the *Wall Street Journal*, we learned from the Vice President of a major wire house:

> "Some institutions also were buying to get more stocks in their portfolios before the end of the quarter. Being invested was the way to look smart (to clients) this quarter," he said.

Only a week later in the same column, investors were advised by the Senior Vice President of the St. Louis office of another major brokerage firm:

> "The relatively low volume lately suggests that many institutional players also are sitting this market out. If you had a real fright in the market, you would see volumes of 120 million to 130 million plus. But we are merely in a lackluster market, and whenever volume dries up, prices slide a bit."

If all this isn't crystal clear, perhaps the October 10 comments by the Senior Executive Vice President of a very large wire house can clarify matters:

> "The market can't sustain a rally temporarily. The problem is that most money managers and the general public are either selling or sitting on the sidelines."

We couldn't agree more. Either the institutions are buying, sitting on their hands, or selling. That about exhausts the possibilities. True, stock market columns can make for good, relaxing *entertainment*, along with sports columns, TV and movie columns, and the like. But they certainly shouldn't be taken as gospel in a matter as serious as investing. As our founder John Magee noted over twenty years ago:

> "Every now and then some stock, a group of stocks, or the whole market, which has been lying dormant for weeks, suddenly takes off in a great explosion of activity...Some people will say, 'Well, there must be a reason in back of this activity.' It may be a good reason, it may be a bad reason, it may be a reason not directly related to the company, but perhaps to politics, international affairs, matters of control or merger of corporations, etc. There could be two reasons, three, many reasons, all true. We prefer to study carefully what is going on in the market, to make our inferences and decisions on that and not to dig too deeply into the rich, confusing veins, arguments, and hypotheses."

CALLING THE TURN:
A CASE OF MISSING THE POINT

Recently, we received a copy of an article "Calling the Turn" which appeared in the August, 1984 issue of *Registered Representative* magazine. Now ordinarily, we pass over such reports, forecasts, predictions, and the like with only the briefest of glances. But in this one case we did hesitate, set aside the article, and attacked it with relish shortly thereafter. After all, "Calling The Turn" is a headline with universal appeal. And we are only human.

The article, it turns out, was really an optimistic assessment of the outlook for natural gas in the United States. "Are we at the Bottom of a classic commodity cycle in natural gas?," asks the subtitle. The author then proceeds to list a number of issues which suggest that, over the long term, a recovery in natural gas prices is likely. Typical of the points raised are that (1) "the depression in drilling activity means we're not replacing the reserves we're using," and (2) "production from existing gas wells is starting to decline very rapidly."

Although the author acknowledges that "natural gas prices are probably not going to get any Major, immediate boost from the crossover between supply and demand," he nevertheless advises Registered Representatives to approach their clients with confidence and simplicity: "I think we've identified a Major turnaround in the, making, and it's got some great earnings potential for investors like you."

Now, our understanding of the meaning of "turning point," at least in the context of stocks and commodities, and the marketplaces in which they trade, is that point at which a change in the Major direction or Trend of *price* occurs. In our view, a recitation of Trends *affecting* the price of a particular stock or commodity really has little or nothing to do with the issue of Calling the Turn of price itself.

A recent case in point, of course, is the behavior of interest rates in the U.S. Certainly, major factors affecting the level of interest rates in the U.S. throughout 1984 were the strong U.S. economy and the huge federal deficit. We are aware of numerous economists and forecasters who based their predictions of further escalating interest rates on these underlying factors which to date remain in force. Yet, since June, there has been a major turning point in Treasury Bills (December 1984), and *decline* in interest rates, as the chart at below illustrates.

We conclude that any article or prediction which heralds a turning point without specifically considering *supply and demand as measured by price and trading activity in the marketplace* is not worth the paper it is printed on. Or, stated another way, no pun intended, we think the authors of articles such as "Calling the Turn" have missed the point entirely.

FIGURE 8

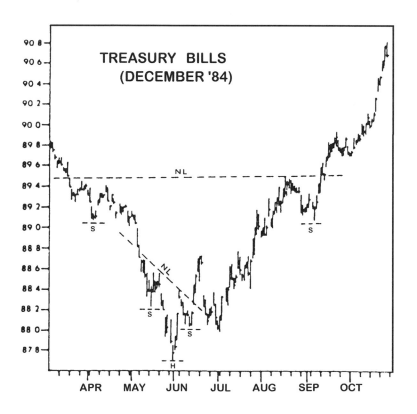

Analyzing Bar Charts for Profit

SUBJECT TO DELAY

Last April, with the stock market in the doldrums and takeover activity consequently on the rise, we had the opportunity to review a favorite technical formation—the "takeover pattern." As illustrations, we presented several "before and after (the takeover announcement) charts," all of companies whose shares soared in price after public announcement of a takeover agreement. We even went so far as to include the chart of Prentice-Hall which clearly showed classic takeover characteristics. On April 13, with PTN at 50 1/4, so unmistakable was the PTN formation that we inserted a question mark above the point where the announcement should occur—a sort of "pre-takeover chart" as it were. Taking note of the classic, extraordinary price and volume activity, we concluded that "significant corporate developments are underway, about which we will learn more shortly."

As noted in our April 14, *Page One*, the telltale pattern consists of "a spike upward on heavy volume, followed by a pullback on light volume; and, after several weeks (usually four to six), a sharp rise, again on very high volume." It was further noted that "the final price/volume drive typically occurs on a *Friday* with the takeover stock *closing* at or near the high of the day's price range."

Imagine our disappointment, then, when PTN did not announce that it was being acquired (or taken over) in late April or early May. Or in July, when it broke our protective limit of 41 1/2 before recording a low of 34 3/8.

Everything became clear two weeks ago, however, after PTN soared five points in heavy trading on Friday, November 2. A merger (perhaps *the* merger) was imminent. By Monday, Gulf & Western Industries had announced a $70 per share tender offer "after trying unsuccessfully for four months to meet with executives of the Englewood Cliffs, New Jersey publisher."

Perhaps they had been trying to meet with PTN management for four months. *The chart says that the initial decision to acquire PTN was reached in April, fully six months ago;* and that in April and May the usual insiders, perhaps the same ones active on Friday, November 2, were busy expressing themselves in the marketplace in classic manner when an acquisition "secret" is not well kept.

FIGURE 9

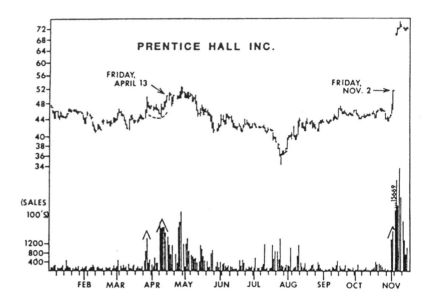

Analyzing Bar Charts for Profit

November 24, 1984

ON PROTECTING ONE'S ASSETS

More than twenty years ago, the young messenger carried his first "white slip" in the boisterous trading room of the prestigious Wall Street brokerage firm. Long and narrow like the control room of a battleship, the trading room was located in the same building that housed the New York Stock Exchange. Both on the floor of the stock exchange and in the trading room, legendary Wall Street traders gathered daily to test their nerves and judgment in the crucible of the world's largest auction market.

The young man's exhilaration at becoming a junior trader was immeasurable; the opportunity to sit next to and learn directly from "The Most Astute Trader in Wall Street" was an unparalleled opportunity.

It was a curious mixture of youthful enthusiasm and seasoned wisdom, and the trainee observed the skillful and masterful trading techniques of his silver-haired mentor. Repeatedly, large trading positions were quietly acquired and then, almost as if by magic, the price of the stock would rise and the position would be sold at a profit.

Each time the young man would also invest a small portion of his savings in the same stock; and over time his assets increased greatly. In fact, so sure did the young man become of the success of his method, and the infallibility of his mentor, that he opened a margin account and took larger and larger positions as his wealth increased.

One day the "opportunity of a lifetime" presented itself. The silver-haired trader quietly began accumulating the stock and by week's end owned a 20,000-share position. The young man stretched his assets to the limit, used all his borrowing power, and by week's end he also owned 20,000 shares. Although it was his only holding, the "usual gain" that he expected would make him very rich. After all, he was following the course set by "the most astute trader in Wall Street."

The ending of this story is familiar. Instead of rising from 20 to 30, the chosen stock fell from 20 to 10. The young man's savings were wiped out and, in fact, a small debit remained on the books. The senior trader added a few gray hairs, commenting something to the effect that "you can't win them all."

But in a brief conversation which followed, a message did go out. "At least," said the young man, "I've learned how not to go broke. I'll never put all my eggs in one basket again."

"No," said the silver-haired trader, "what you've learned about is only *one way* not to go broke. There are an *infinite* number of other ways to go broke; in fact, there is always one more way."

We have long counseled our subscribers on the dangers of "leveraging" with borrowed funds, and on the advantages of diversifying their assets by size and by industry. Our method of rigorous observation of protective limits further protects each investment position on an individual basis. The surest way to prepare for substantial gains is first to defend successfully against substantial losses. This has been our guiding philosophy for over two decades of advising investors.

December 15, 1984

THE ELLIOTT WAVE THEORY: PERSPECTIVE AND COMMENTS

This week we had the pleasure of attending the December meeting of the Market Technicians Association of New York. Long-term subscribers will remember the MTANY as the organization which honored John Magee with its "Man of the Year" award in 1978. The speaker was Robert Prechter, publisher of "The Elliott Wave Theorist," an investment advisory which bases its forecasts on interpretations of R.N. Elliott's work on the stock market. Readers can tell at a glance where Prechter thinks the stock market stands currently (see Figure 10).

Of primary interest to SAS subscribers are Prechter's comments on technical analysis itself. The Elliott Wave Theory, it must be remembered, is really no more than a "catalog" of stock market price movements, laid one on top of the other, so to speak, until a grand, underlying and enduring pattern is observed; in short, pure *technical* analysis. Among Prechter's definitions and observations regarding fundamental analysis are the following:

1. "First let's define 'technical' versus 'fundamental' data ...technical data is that which is generated by the action of the market under study."

2. "The main problem with fundamental analysis is that its indicators are removed from the market itself. The analyst assumes causality between external events and market movements, a concept which is almost certainly false...But, just as important, and less recognized, is that fundamental analysis almost always requires a *forecast of the fundamental data itself* before conclusions about the market are drawn. The analyst is then forced to take a *second* step in coming to a conclusion about how those forecasted events will affect the markets! Technicians only have one step to take, which gives

them an edge right off the bat. Their main advantage is that they don't have to forecast their indicators."

3. "What's worse, even the fundamentalists' second step is probably a process built on quicksand...The most common application of fundamental analysis is estimating companies' earnings for both the current year and next year, and recommending stocks on that basis ...And the record on that basis alone is very poor, as *Barron's* pointed out in a June 4 article, which showed that earnings estimates averaged 18% error in the thirty DJIA stocks for any year already completed and 54% error for the year ahead. The weakest link, however, is the assumption that correct earnings estimates are a basis for choosing stock market winners. According to a table in the same *Barron's* article, a purchase of the ten DJIA stocks with the best earnings estimates would have produced a ten-year cumulative gain of 40.5%, while choosing the ten DJIA with the worst earnings estimates would have produced a whopping 142.5% gain."

We enjoyed Prechter's polished exposition of a technical approach different from our own. As for his observations about fundamental analysis, we simply couldn't agree more.

FIGURE 10

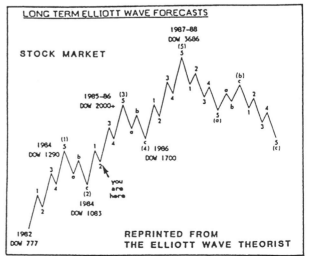

Analyzing Bar Charts for Profit

FIGURE 11

WHEN A STOCK COLLAPSES: CRISIS OR OPPORTUNITY?

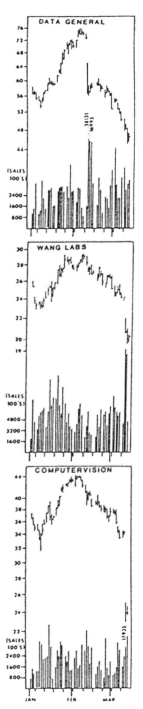

In recent weeks, holders of several big-name technology stocks have been subjected to the agony of a "delayed opening —news pending" announcement followed by a severe decline in the market price of their shares. It all began four weeks ago when Data General announced that "current-quarter earnings could be below expectations of Wall Street analysts." From its Monday, February 11 closing price of 72 7/8. DGN collapsed to an intra-day low of 56 1/2 before recovering to close at 58 3/4, off 14 1/8 for the day.

On Tuesday of this week, holders of Wang Labs were subjected to a spine chilling decline of approximately equal proportions, as were holders of Computervision (see Figure 11) on Wednesday when that company predicted "breakeven results on less-than-expected sales" for the current quarter. For Wang, the drop amounted to 9 3/8 points. The one-day 9 3/4-point plunge in CVN (to 23 7/8) amounted to an astounding $270 million reduction (one-third) of that company's market value.

While the above events constituted a crisis for existing holders of Data General, Wang, and Computervision, they represent unfolding opportunity for the balance of the investing public. Just as computer and technology stocks were the "darlings" of the 1982-83 stock market rally, and are today its "black sheep," many of these issues will undoubtedly score large advances from current levels. In Wall Street, the wheel turns.

Technical analysis is unusually well-suited for such occasions. First, no technical tenet would justify Bottom-picking, or buying into a decline" such as those currently underway in DGN. WANB, and CVN. Often such declines are precursors to substantial further declines. What technical analysis requires after such a jarring decline is a settling down or cooling-off period. Typically, these last a minimum of three weeks and as long as several months. And typically, the Bottoming process after such drastic declines involves a series of recognizable events—a rally of 30% to 50% of the preceding decline followed by a low volume test of the "crisis" low. The final configuration of the basing process—Head-and-Shoulders, Rectangle, or Double Bottom—cannot be ascertained in advance. One thing is clear, however, most of today's fallen angels will be available at current prices or lower for some time to come. And when the Trend is about to reverse, that fact will be evident on the daily price and volume chart. Corporate announcements, as so clearly shown this week, simply do not occur in time to be useful for investor decision-making.

ACQUISITIONS FEVER REVISITED

FIGURE 12

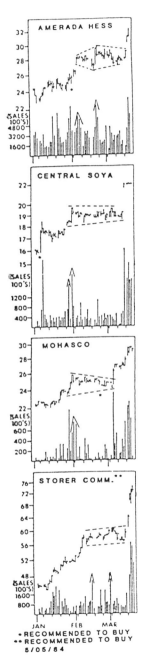

The Magee list of open long positions has been fertile territory for takeover stocks in recent weeks. Last week's takeover winner, Central Soya (sold this week for a 32.1% gain) was completely overshadowed by American Broadcasting Company (recommended to buy on December 15, 1984 at 62). After gaining 2 1/8 points last Friday on heavy volume, ABC gapped open on Monday, from Capital Cities Communication. Other open long positions soaring 31 3/8 points to 105 7/8 in response to a takeover proposal benefitting from specific or rumored takeover developments this week were Amerada Hess, Mohasco, and Storer Communications. Charts of each stock clearly revealed the price/volume characteristics we have long associated with the pre-takeover behavior first described in our March 18, 1978 *Page One* ("Acquisition Fever"), and reviewed again in September of that year. The typical pre-takeover pattern was described as one in which:

1. Volume soared;

2. A pullback to Support followed on relatively low volume; and

3. Both volume and price resumed their Uptrends four to six weeks later, immediately prior to the takeover announcement. Gains of 50% to 100% typically followed such announcements.

We even developed a theory to explain this chart pattern: "When a takeover is conceived, it is first communicated to a small group of corporate officials at the highest level, usually (but not always) on both sides of the proposed transaction. If an agreement is possible (or a takeover struggle likely), that information passes either explicitly or implicitly to a very small group of immediate associates of the principals involved in the initial discussions. *Some amount of stock is bought based on that information, often quite urgently* (i.e., the first "spike" of our "typical pattern"). The public, unaware of such going-ons, jumps at the opportunity to take profits, and shares of the potential takeover candidate drop back to their previous price level *on low volume.* Three or four weeks go by. A select (but larger) group of professionals works on the proposed transaction, from lawyers and printers to secretaries and investment bankers, all sworn to secrecy. A memorandum of agreement is drawn up. At about the time it is in final form, ready for signing, a second, larger, and very urgent spike develops, on very high volume. The stock exchange is then requested to suspend trading in XYZ common stock pending an important announcement.

As can be seen from Figure 12—the chart ABC is excluded for space reasons—very little has changed since our initial observations. Of course, not all takeovers leave telltale footprints on the charts. *Sometimes secrets are perfectly kept.* But to the extent that they are not, technical analysis is a powerful (and relatively safe) tool for seeking out likely buyout candidates. Presently, there are 134 open positions on our master list of long recommendations, pages 5 through 7, not counting the five issues mentioned above. Good hunting!

AN EASY WAY TO BUY A PILE OF TROUBLE

This weekend we overheard a particularly interesting conversation. A new investor (a very likeable chap) had a great idea. "Buy Oak Industries," he advised. "Interest rates are coming down, and that should be good for the stock. Besides it's selling for less than half its price three months ago and has to be really cheap here."

Some years back, when we were new in this business, we had a similar idea. If we took several well-known stocks, say a half a dozen, and followed their daily price fluctuations, we could make a sure profit simply by buying one or two of the stocks that had gone down in price, and selling or selling short one or two of them that had gone up. Then as the depressed ones recovered, we could sell them; and as the advancing ones had a bit of a reaction, we could cover our short sales. Thus, while the profits would be limited, the transactions would be relatively easy to carry out successfully and we would be making a small gain on balance.

Luckily, we had the good sense or good fortune to try this scheme out on paper before actually putting any hard money into it because it did not work out very well. Somehow the stocks that were breaking down and we purchased, too often, it seemed, continued to go right on down. And the ones that had moved up seemed to continue up some more. We tried dividing our capital into several parts, and buying more stock on the way down, or selling more stock short on the way up. But "averaging down", as it is called, did not work either. In fact, if we had followed that procedure, we would have been very broke, indeed, and very soon.

As we learned more about the market, we found that there were a number of well-known plans based on the general idea of averaging down. As we got deeper into our study, we discovered that none of these methods offered the sure, easy way to fame and fortune that we had hoped for.

We think a useful repudiation of this sort of approach can be found in a book of long-term stock charts, showing price Trends over a period of some years. As you may already know, or as you will see, the stocks that are moving into new all-time high ground frequently continue moving up in value for months and years; and those that are in the sub-basement often tend to stay there a long time, or move lower.

We would rather buy a stock that has completed a Reversal Pattern and is *already on its way up.* In the typical case, after languishing for several months in a narrow pattern, a stock breaks through Resistance on the Upside, in heavy trading. On the pullback to Support, the odds have moved heavily into our favor and limit protection is excellent.

Allied Stores, Electronics Corporation of America, and Sterling Drug strike us as particularly attractive purchase candidates at this time—ones whose stock charts clearly say that things are improving at the corporate level, rather than vice versa.

Common sense tells us that Reversals in direction take time, *if they occur at all.* Which is why we like to buy or sell short *after* the Major Trend is in place, even if it costs us a bit more to enter the game.

THE FIRST SHOE DROPS

A few weeks back, at the invitation of *Barron's* we penned an article about the classic technical pattern which often precedes corporate takeovers, or takeover-related activities. Entitled, "Worth a Thousand Words," the *Barron's* May 6, 1985 article highlighted four companies "whose charts exhibit classic pre-takeover patterns but for which no takeover has (yet) been announced." The four companies were Allied Stores, Amerada Hess, Time and United Brands.

When contacted by *Barron's,* spokesmen for Allied Stores, Time and United Brands were quick to deny any knowledge about pending takeover, or takeover-related activities. "We are not talking to anybody," said Orren Knauer, an Allied Vice President. Time spokesman, Louis Slovinsky, reported that "the company isn't talking to any suitors," and that the company had "put in some anti-takeover provisions such as staggered election of directors." Even more specific was the spokeswoman for Carl Linder's American Financial Corporation which, according to *Barron's,* owned 58% of United Brands' stock. "There have been no talks either about buying the rest of the stock or about selling American Financial's stake," she declared. As for Amerada Hess, it failed to return *Barron's* phone call.

Imagine our surprise on Friday of this week, then, when a company called FMI Financial offered to buy four million shares of United Brands at 20. FMI Financial, the news release went on to say, is controlled by Carl Lindner, principal shareholder in both American Financial and United Brands.

Return for a moment to the UB chart shown in *Barron's.* To the date of the article, the United Brands chart contained "no less than five Friday spikes, an extraordinary number in our experience," we reported. Add to that the current offer to purchase four million shares made on July 5—also a Friday! An astounding coincidence, we are sure.

We have often referred to technical analysis as the art of following footsteps on the charts. Price and volume data do reflect the activities of "informed players," as well as all others; and these often do provide unmistakable clues to impending events. Certainly, this was the case with United Brands. The jury is still out in the matters of Allied Stores, Amerada Hess, and Time. Which shoe will drop next?

FIGURE 13

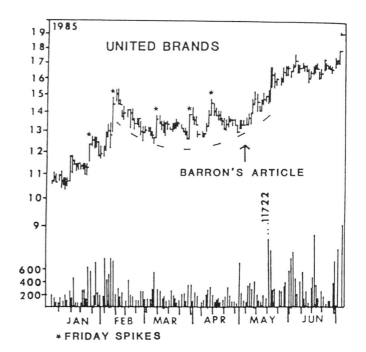

PROTECTING STOCK MARKET PROFITS or
A TRIP INTO THE WILD BLUE YONDER AND BACK

Except for the names (which have been changed), this is a true story about a woman investor we know who got wind of a big move coming up in Blue Yonder Computer Corporation. According to rumors, the company had developed a new process by which it could store the King James version of the Holy Bible on a memory chip the size of your eyelash, and major production was just around the corner. In June, 1983, Linda High Hopes bought 2,000 shares of Blue Yonder stock for 80 cents each, or $1,600; not an in ordinate amount to place in an extremely speculative stock.

Those around the office, however, shook their heads. How many times had they heard about impressive new products, discoveries, or processes, all in connection with low-price (penny) stocks—only to see the bubble burst in the dawn's early light?

They weren't even particularly impressed when Blue Yonder rose to $1.20 a share in July, a heady 50% advance in thirty days. They were even more impressed, moreover, when Linda called up and bought another 1,000 shares at $1.25.

Their indifference turned to profound respect (and a little bit of envy) the following year when Blue Yonder reached $2.80, at which price their friend bought 2,000 additional shares (June), and then when she purchased another 2,000 shares in December at $4.00. By early this year Linda had accumulated 7,000 shares at an average cost of $2.46 per share. Her unrealized gain approached $30,000 this spring as Blue Yonder traded above $6.00 on the NASDAQ National Market.

Along the way, Linda's broker suggested she sell half her holdings (thereby getting her investment back plus a considerable gain), while "letting her profits run on the balance of the position." The advice was received politely, but not acted upon. And Blue Yonder, which had previously been something of an erratic performer, settled down into a long holding pattern at $6.00. Then in a short period of time, Blue Yonder sold off sharply, dropping to $3.60 a share where it again held briefly. No, Linda was not disturbed by this weakness, nor did she ask for quotes on a daily basis any longer. It had become a long-term holding.

Imagine everyone's surprise, however, when Linda's broker received a phone call to sell 7,000 shares of Blue Yonder last week. We punched out BYON on the quote machine. It was selling for $1.20 per share! After some consultation, Linda decided to hold her shares a bit longer, not a bad decision based on their recent price of $1.80. Her loss, if she sold today would be less than $5,000—not overly damaging in the world of high finance. But the foregone profits of nearly $30,000 are a great loss. *To be successful as an investor, one must learn how to realize profits as well as how to protect against major losses.*

In our service we have noted repeatedly that investors are continually subjected to information, rumors, and tips of every sort—most of them well-intended. And that unless each investor develops his or her own philosophy with regard to buying and selling, he or she will be unable to operate successfully in the stock market. In the case of Linda High Hopes and Blue Yonder, simple maintenance of a daily chart, attention to Trendlines, and a firm resolve to "get out of a stock once it turns weak," would have made all the difference.

THE HEMLINE BAROMETER AND OTHER "MOOD" MEASURES AS CRYSTAL BALLS TO THE FUTURE

"The market price reflects not only differing value opinions of many orthodox security appraisers, but also all the hopes and fears and guesses and moods, rational and irrational, of hundreds of potential buyers and sellers, as well as their needs and their resources—in total, factors which defy analysis and for which no statistics are obtainable, but which are nevertheless all synthesized, weighed and finally expressed in the one precise figure at which a buyer and seller get together and make a deal."

—*Technical Analysis of Stock Trends*
by Robert D. Edwards and John Magee

Followers of Edwards and Magee are familiar with the basic tenets of the pattern recognition school of technical analysis, particularly the hard-to-measure psychological bias which underlies the individual trader's decision-making process. Fundamentalists can argue about rational, fact-filled reasons to buy or sell. But clearly, the emotional state of the investing public is a major factor in the movement of the stock market. As chartists, we are constantly attempting to measure these changes with systematic analysis of price and volume. On a broader scale, however, an astute observer can also anticipate changes in the basic emotional foundation of the public by observing popular culture itself, a sort of "stepping back from the trees to look at the forest" approach.

Although this is not a new, or even a surprising, theory, we had not given the matter much thought—aside from a chuckle or two over using the "Hemline" barometer as a measure of Bullishness—until we read a recent article (*Barron's*, September 9, 1985) by Robert Prechter of Elliott Wave fame. Apparently, there is more than a shapely calf to meet the eye in hemlines and other changes in public taste. Indeed, Mr. Prechter postulates that popular art, fashion and mores reflect the dominant public mood and that the stock market, being a highly reflective arena of emotional behavior, moves in concert with these major shifts in public attitude. He further suggests that these dominant moods, whether negative or positive, have a great deal to do with the character, and are *possibly the cause*, of historic events. "Major historic events which are often considered important to the future (i.e., economic activity, law making, war) are not causes of change: they are the result of mass mood changes which have already occurred." If this is so, then one can argue, as Mr. Prechter does, that "...evidence of mood change is the *single most important* area of discovery for those who wish to peek into the future of fundamental events. In the world of popular culture, 'trendsetters' and the avant garde must be watched closely since their ideas are often an expression of the leading edge of public mood."

The article goes on to point out how fashion, movies, and, particularly, popular music tastes have signaled Major turning points in the stock market over the past 35 years. These observations will not help a short- or intermediate-term trader much, nor will it aid you in timing a specific stock position. But, as a broad measure of the general health of a long-term Trend, it has merit. Incidentally, by Mr. Prechter's reading of the popular culture barometer, we appear to be in a period akin to the mid-1920s.

For further information on this subject, we refer you to New Classics Library, Inc., P.O. Box 1618, Gainesville, GA 30503.

AN OVERSOLD MARKET

This week, the Magee Evaluative Index fell to 9% Strong, its deepest penetration into the oversold quadrant this year. Not since June of 1984 has this index been lower (see Figure 14). Shortly after its June low of 8% Strong, the MEI headed steadily higher, giving an Aggressive Buy signal throughout late June and July.

The June 1984 MEI low of 8% Strong, together with the 8% level reached on February 25, 1984, constituted a Double Bottom oversold reading for this index. It corresponded to the 1079 Bottom recorded by the Dow Jones Industrial Average on June 18, 1984, after which that index advanced steadily to its recent July peak of 1372 (see Figure 14).

For over twenty years, all major stock market Bottoms have corresponded with extremely low MEI readings. During the "turbulent period" when the stock market oscillated violently but showed no gain at all, MEI readings of 5% Strong or less corresponded with all Major DJIA Bottoms until the June 1982 low of 9% Strong, which immediately preceded the stock market's upward explosion.

That slightly higher than "5% Strong or less" Bottom was an important clue that a reinvigorated stock market was at hand; the straight-line DJIA advance from 770 to nearly 1300 ended a 17-year "do-nothing" period for stock prices and ushered in the "renewed upswing" period shown on the chart.

In this context, the "8% Strong Bottom" of June, 1984, and the current MEI reading of 9% Strong, take on added meaning. If, in fact, we are in a period of Renewed (or major secular) Upswing, stock market Bottoms will tend to be less severe—and Tops more extremely overbought, than would otherwise be the case. Both the June, 1982 DJIA low and that of June, 1984 fit this model. Because secular stock market waves tend to last for many years—even decades—the likelihood is that the current MEI reading of 9% Strong will also define a Major DJIA low.

FIGURE 14

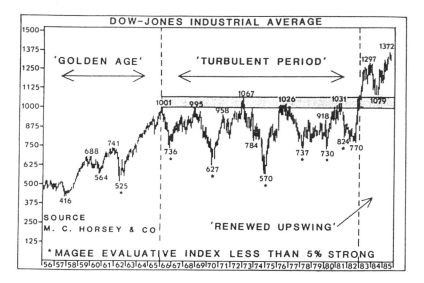

148

...AND HOW HIGH DO YOU THINK IT WILL GO?

With the Dow Jones Industrial Average near 1500, and 130-million-share days commonplace, America's favorite indoor sport is pursued once again: predicting the market. Each day we get phone calls from clients, prospective clients, former clients, and other friends who so often ask, "...and how high do you think it will go?" Most of the people we know well are prepared for the answer, the only answer we have ever given: "We haven't the slightest idea...."

It is not that we don't have some definite ideas about stocks and about the market as a whole; for we pride ourselves on the definitive recommendations we make. But we do not state predictions in the terms so many people use. Nobody knows, we feel, just exactly what will happen in domestic or world affairs next week or next month. So far as we are aware, nobody car pinpoint the "objective" or the duration of a move in the market quantitatively, without hedging it around with a lot of "ifs," "ands," and "buts."

However, we know that we have liked numerous stocks over the past year including such issues as Storer Broadcasting, CAP, Inc., Pepsico, I-ICA, and Woolworth (F.W.), all with gains of 70% to more than 150% since recommendation. And that the beleaguered high-tech sector, prominently featured over the past few weeks, erupted this week with further substantial gains likely. But how high they will go or how long they will continue to act well; that we don't know. It all depends on the many factors that can affect the future condition of the market; and these can change rapidly in today's volatile financial environment.

We can recognize that there is some weakness in this stock or that one, and still understand that there are not many, even now, that are showing great weakness even with the Magee Evaluative Index in the "overbought" quartile. The idea is to be in a flexible position, ready to get out with the least amount of damage in case conditions change suddenly.

There is no harm in conversation as conversation. It may make a good accompaniment to a hot cup of coffee or a dry martini. People can spend hours discussing philosophy or religion or the new politics of the right, and, just so they don't become too deeply involved at the operational level, no one is hurt. In the same way, wherever a few people are gathered together, one is likely to hear heated discussion about the President's speech, or the next OPEC meeting, or why the decline in wheat prices is going to shoot stock prices up or knock them down (depending on what the speaker happens to own and what he wants to happen). After two cups of hot coffee or three martinis, some of them will begin pounding on the table and offering side bets that the averages will hit 1600 before December 31, or that IBM will advance to 150 before April 1. And this can hurt if a person begins to believe all this. He or she will "project" the action of a few stocks, or of some average or index, and then act as though this projection would "pull the others" along with it. This is not good predicting.

We must, of course, make plans and act on them. But none of us can aspire to divine wisdom. Sometimes it is enough to say simply, "*This* stock looks strong to me *now*." This leaves the matter of revision open without prejudice.

Analyzing Bar Charts for Profit

THE STOCK MARKET: NOT SO RANDOM

A very interesting theory which has always fascinated us concerns the so-called Random Walk explanation of stock prices. We assume that a drunk emerges from the tavern in the wee hours, and heads for home. That is to say, he would head for home, his intention is to proceed home, but his sense of direction has been altered (or obliterated) by his copious ingestion of C_2H_5OH. He gets as far as the center of the square where there is a lamp post on the cement "island." This gives him support to gather his energies for the homeward journey.

With no sense of direction, our friend will tend to zig-zag in a series of random moves, unfortunately carrying him back and forth and from side to side of the square, but sadly not getting him any closer to hearth and home. Except that in the course of the zigging and the zagging he may very well move for a time in what seems to be a consistent direction. Eventually, the theory continues, his moves will "cancel out" and he will sooner or later stagger right into the lamp post again.

This may very well be true of drunks in a public square. We are quite sure, despite the arguments of some notable theoreticians to the contrary, that it does not apply to the behavior of stock price movements, weather conditions, or actuarial risks in insurance. As a matter of fact if stock price movements were "truly" random in the sense of the home-seeking drunk, no method of prediction, technical, fundamental, or what have you would be of any value whatsoever. One might just as well pick one's stock portfolio by dropping the names of the stocks in a hat and picking them blindfolded.

It is rather hard, however, to pick up a copy of *The Wall Street Journal*, and look at their chart of the well-known Dow Jones Industrials on the next-to-last page, and say, "This is a meaningless ramble; it could be a chart of the lurching progress of friend drunk." Certainly the advance from September

18 through this week hardly looks like an inebriated walk. It is very consistently up.

A stock called GAP, Inc. on the Big Board has risen over 200% in value in the past year. MCA held firm in a 9-month horizontal move through February then broke topside. Since then it has risen 60% in a relentless stairstep Uptrend. Look at the 1985 Trends in Pepsico (up); in Woolworth (up); and McDermott (down). These hardly look random, like a drunk walking, or like spinning a roulette wheel, or flipping a coin. No, they reflect, we believe, the underlying "fundamental" factors which, actually, we do not need to know in detail, the charts themselves tell the story.

We haven't encountered a "random walk" theorist for some time. They used to show up here from time to time and we had some great old arguments. They are probably right, in a sense. Probably no one can "predict" the extent or duration of a Trend. But one surely can tell that Northern Indiana Public Service is in trouble here, and that NCR is doing very well thank you. When the market goes somewhere it doesn't stagger; it usually heads straight off for wherever it is going. Which is the basis of almost everything we do here at John Magee Inc.

PROFESSIONAL OBSOLESCENCE

Most of us who are over 30 have a sneaking suspicion that if we went back to school, we might have a harder time making it through. Nowadays, pre-school children are learning the alphabet while watching Sesame Street. What will these children do when they reach kindergarten, where learning the ABCs used to be standard fare? Remember the flash cards?

And so it is right up the educational ladder. Seventh graders learn geometry; high school students calculus; and, Lord knows, what complex theories of sets, games, quantum this's and molecular thats, confront students in the ordinary course of a college education today.

Now with all this knowledge drummed into us from day one, we should be well equipped to cope with the rigors of modern-day professional life, we thought.

Not so.

A while back we read a study by a professor of psychology at Pennsylvania State University. According to the learned Doctor, most of us are probably obsolete in our professions at this very time. Five years out of college, he suggests, an engineer may be obsolete. Other examples of speedy obsolescence: five years for medical internists, five to ten years for computer technologists, ten years or less for psychologists, etc.

Stated another way, an engineering graduate, class of 1970, presently commands only 43% of the applicable knowledge in his field. For the class of 1960, the figure drops to 37%; and for 1955, 19%. And so on for internists, computer technologists, psychologists, and stock market forecasters.

Stock market forecasters? Does the professor maintain that if we have been forecasting stock price behavior since 1955 we are 81% obsolete?

When it comes to analyzing the behavior of a stock we believe that *experience*, not knowledge of the latest "techniques," is the key to successful investing. Nothing, in our view, substitutes for meticulous, repetitive analysis of the ever-changing patterns of common stock price and volume behavior.

A Flag here, a Pennant there, reduced volume on an up day, a close at the high on heavy volume—the experienced technical analyst will notice these particular events, measure them against the breadth of his accumulated experience, and make his recommendation.

Since when do clocks run backwards?

February 1, 1986

WE WOULD NOT WANT TO GET SCARED OUT OF THE MARKET TOO SOON

We note that a highly regarded colleague, a technician in fact, has likened the recent "widely publicized 52-point shakeout in the Dow Industrials" to "the stock market's performance in early 1946. In February of that year," he states, "the Dow Industrials declined...following that February 1946 shakeout, the Dow Industrials recovered by late May before beginning a 23% decline by the final quarter of 1946." He concludes that, "I believe investors should be prepared for at least the type of declines witnessed in 1946, and on six occasions during the past two decades."

There is no doubt that riding herd on a portfolio of stocks, especially in an active and sharply advanced market, is a tense, nerve-wracking business. We have often noted that the owners of stocks that are going up in price rapidly seem to suffer more anxiety that the holders of stocks that are going down in a Bear Market. Apparently, the threat is mainly to the ego. It is always possible to rationalize holding a stock as it topples and slides to new lows. One can buy more of it, "average" the cost, accumulate stock at "bargain prices," and undoubtedly defend it loyally with optimistic predictions by the Chairman of the Board.

But when a stock is going up by leaps and bounds, the strain on its owner seems unbearable. To sell it after a 20-point rise...and then see it continue up another 20 points (like Union Carbide recently)...can hurt one's self-regard. And to hang onto it, and then have it crumble and sag and fall to pieces before one's eyes, can also hurt (like Storage Technology last year).

So, it is no wonder that there are so many worried-looking people pacing up and down at the back of board rooms these days. They are the investors who happen to be holding one or more profitable stocks which have advanced at a rapid clip and on which they are holding a substantial profit.

It might be easier on the nerves, and, ultimately, on the pocketbook, if these investors faced the question as a problem in probabilities. He or she might ask whether there was any evidence to date that the particular stock was weakening, and whether this evidence was sufficient to justify selling it. Or, quite reasonably, after a big run-up, decide to put a close stop order just below the previous day's close, so as to gain the benefit of any further straight-line advance, but to be safely out in case of the slightest reaction. This would mean, to be sure, sacrificing the ultimate hope of maximum long-term gains if the Trend were interrupted by a normal period of reaction and then continued up. But it would represent a positive decision and, for some, it might be worth the possible loss of future profits to be "off the hook."

Or the investor might continue to hold the stock through any "normal" reaction, until or unless it showed symptoms of a Major Reversal, and then sell it summarily. Although such an approach never captures the extreme of any move, holdings retained until a Major Reversal occurs often yield very large capital gains.

Discomfort is a normal component of speculating, which is what all investment really is. Whichever investment approach one follows, it surely helps to understand the element of uncertainty which is part of the picture; and to realize that buy or sell decisions made on a stock-by-stock basis have a better chance of working out well than do dramatic across-the-board decisions to buy or sell all stocks because "the DJIA is about to go up (or down) 50 points."

HOLE IN ONE

No sane golfer would announce his or her intention of making a hole-in-one this afternoon on the next hole. Yet, with increasing frequency, we hear about investors, flush with recent stock market gains, who are "taking a big position" in this or that stock and who expect to "make a killing."

Of course, everyone can *hope* for a hole-in-one, or to make a stock market killing. Try their best and all that. If a duffer, or a tyro, their chances are pretty small. And even expert golfers know that this is something that *happens*; if the stance is right, if the drive is clean, if one is in top form and not upset or rattled; and if one is lucky besides. After all, the slightest puff of wind could deflect the most perfect drive. There is skill involved, and one should not deprecate the achievement. But there is also luck.

Although most people, consciously or unconsciously, realize that holes-in-one require a combination of good golf and good luck, it is strange how many people go out to play a *much tougher game than golf* for the first time in their lives, set their ball up on the tee, whack it down the fairway or into the woods, and then wonder why they didn't make a hole-in-one. They go into the stock market on a gamble, tip, or rumor, staking savings they cannot afford to lose on the most speculative stocks, without diversification or predetermined loss limits.

There are people sitting day after day, month after month, in many brokers' boardrooms, watching the Trans-Lux, making small commitments in this stock or that. And someone may point out one of these to you, and tell you, "That is, Bill so-and-so. He loaded up on PQR ten years ago and made a killing. Parlayed his margin account right up to a million and half dollars in three months. But he tried it again the next year on XYZ and lost it all in about the same time."

Then, we have the market forecasters warning their subscribers to "Sell everything and go short," that "the DJIA is headed for a sharp selloff;" or advising that the stock market is headed "straight up." Common sense suggests neither forecast will be "right," yet many investors follow their "leaders" without question, as if satisfactory results were guaranteed.

Champion golfers do not depend on holes-in-one or "all or nothing" drives. Successful investors do not depend on "lucky breaks" to convert excessively margined, speculative positions to "once in a lifetime" profits. Successful people depend on methods which can advance their interests in good times and also protect their interests in hard times. Like bridge players making the most of the cards they hold, good or bad.

In this era of dramatic stock market gains we hope there will not be too many would-be wizards of Wall Street who will rush in armed with market orders and stop orders to show that they, too, can make a hole-in-one once they have received the word from on high.

UP TRENDLINE REVIEW

In light of the fact that the predominant chart pattern in the stocks which comprise the Magee Evaluative Index (roughly 1000 ASE and NYSE issues) is the Uptrend and its close cousin the Up Channel, we felt a review of these important Trendlines is in order. The sharp break in the DJIA was also a contributing factor since the across-the-board retreat in many issues has or will threaten their respective Uptrends.

Uptrend lines in time, are broken—sometimes shortly after being established. The problem for the technician is to decide which breakdowns are of important technical significance, and which are of no practical consequence, i.e., minor penetrations which require a redrafting of the Trendline. Unfortunately, there isn't a surefire way to tell. Some penetrations cannot be determined without confirmation from other chart developments. Experience is also an important factor. *But without exception, penetrations of Trendlines are cause for concern, and do require your immediate attention when they occur*. The decisive penetration of an Intermediate Uptrend Line (IUT), for example, signals that the advance has run out of momentum which, in turn, suggests it may be time for the investor/trader to sell out the issue. A decision to go short, on the other hand, would rest on the subsequent pattern development. A Reversal pattern which forms a small Topping pattern, well away from the IUT, might well be ignored if there is room for the pattern target to be reached before the IUT would be broken. One developing after an IUT breakdown would indicate valid short-selling opportunity.

As a start, we would recommend the following factors be considered when evaluating Uptrend Lines and their possible Reversals. In general, there are three primary tests of authority to use in estimating the importance of an Uptrend Line. The first is the number of Bottoms that have developed at or near the Trendline as the stock has ebbed and flowed. With each successive "test", the significance of the Trendline is increased.

The second factor to look at is the length of time the Trendline has held without an important penetration (the size of the breakdown is covered below) ; naturally, the longer it is, the greater its technical merit and the more important the breakdown. Lastly, the angle (from the horizontal) must be judged. Although how steep is steep is not easily defined, you will find that the greater the angle the less valid the penetration. Basically, flatter Trendlines tend to hold more technical significance when broken. (Note: This is particularly relevant to the current breakdown in the market.)

Once you have decided that you have an important Trendline in place, the next consideration will be the "validity of penetration." This, too, can be broken down into three observable areas. The first issue is the size (percentage) of the breakdown. To be decisive, prices must not only push through the line but close beyond it by a margin equal to about 3% of the stock's price. The second and third considerations refer to volume. If you get a 3% breakdown and trading activity is light, that is all right. You don't need big volume to accompany the decline. Where volume is especially predictive is in the 1% to 3% breakdowns, followed by a modest rally (the so-called throwbacks). If there is no pickup in volume then the situation is critical and the slightest signoff renewed selling pressure may be taken as a signal that the Uptrend has been decisively broken.

As Edwards and Magee point out in *Technical Analysis of Stock Trends*, you cannot apply these rules to Uptrend Lines without a "modicum of judgement." Nor will these Uptrend Lines show the precision of pattern formations in their lower boundary lines. But they are powerful warning signals that the time to react is near.

HEAD-AND-SHOULDERS: A CONTINUING TRADITION

Whenever a Head-and-Shoulders pattern is mentioned, the normal reaction is to expect a Top or Bottom. These are, of course, two of the more reliable Reversal formations. But the *Head-and-Shoulders pattern does not always mean a Reversal*. In one form of the well-known technical pattern, it signals a Continuation of the prevailing Trend. Named the Head-and-Shoulders Consolidation in *Technical Analysis of Stock Trends* by Robert D. Edwards and John Magee, we generally refer to it as a Head-and-Shoulders Continuation because of its Trend implication (Note: A Consolidation is neither fish nor fowl until a breakout and, therefore, does not imply a probable direction as does a Flag or Wedge).

The Head-and-Shoulders Continuation is relatively easy to see and not likely to be confused with a Reversal Head-and-Shoulders pattern because *it is inverted*. That is, an upside Head-and-Shoulders Continuation is essentially a Head-and-Shoulders Bottom formed after a rally (where a Top would be expected if a Reversal was in place), while a Downside Head-and-Shoulders Continuation looks like a Head-and-Shoulders Top, but develops after a decline. However, because these formations tend to be more compressed, i.e., thinner, than their Reversal cousins, they can be confused with a Rectangle.

This pattern can differ in another significant way—volume. In a *Reversal Head-and-Shoulders*, Left Shoulder trading activity is generally the highest, followed by Head volume and flat Right Shoulder volume before the Neckline penetration. For the Continuation variety, volume *can diminish on all three peaks* (or troughs for an upside pattern). Breakout volume, however, is similar to the Reversal formation. The formula for estimating the minimum advance or decline following a breakout is also similar to the Reversal pattern. Measure from the Apex or Apogee of the Head back to the part of the Neckline which crosses directly under the Head. This amount is then added (or subtracted for lower objectives) to the price of the stock where the Neckline penetration occurs. As we mentioned earlier, Head-and-Shoulders Continuation patterns tend to be on the narrow side when compared to Head-and-Shoulders Top or Bottom Reversals. *This means that minimum objectives in the former are exceeded more often than in the latter and are of less value.*

A real-time example of the Head-and-Shoulders Continuation pattern can be found in Community Psychiatric Centers or General Mills (not illustrated). The rally off the February low in CMY was followed by a reaction beginning in early May. The pullback uncovered Support in mid-June at 27 3/4 which launched a rally to near-term Resistance in the 30 area. CMY consolidated for two weeks and penetrated Resistance on heavy volume on its way to new highs in early July. From May to June, however, the tell-tale three prongs of a Head-and-Shoulders formation were in evidence. Volume, in this case, confirmed the Reversal pattern. *But CMY was well off its February low and in an Uptrend* before the irregular Consolidation began. Clearly a Continuation pattern was in progress rather than an indeterminate Consolidation greatly increasing the probability of an upside breakout.

FIGURE 15

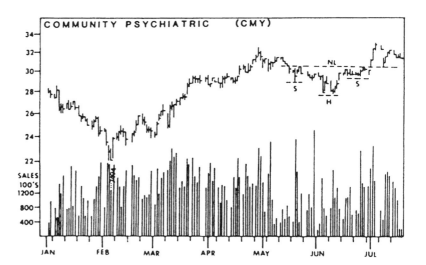

162

THE ROUNDING TURN—
A BIRD WORTH CATCHING

One of the premier Reversal formations in the pattern recognition school of technical analysis is the Head-and-Shoulders Bottom or Top. Sometimes these patterns become quite complex with several Head-and-Shoulders clearly delineated during the construction period. There is another powerful Reversal pattern which can develop as an extension of a series of complex Head-and-Shoulders formations. This is the Rounding Bottom or Top (see *Technical Analysis of Stock Trends*, by Robert D. Edwards and John Magee).

Also called a Bowl (Inverted Bowl for a Top) or a Saucer, this pattern merges small *less violent* Head-and-Shoulders patterns into a string which, over a period of time, shows the progressive change in balance from one force at the beginning to a opposing force at the end. In other words, Rounding Turns reflect the slowly shifting, usually symmetrical, changes in the balance of power between buyers and sellers. Ordinarily, these Rounding patterns take months to evolve and the sharp advance/decline at the end of the turn which confirms the Reversal does not continue very long before a period of Consolidation sets in. Indeed, the Trend change which follows is apt to be *slow and interrupted frequently with corrections and Consolidations.* The latter, moreover, can take on the rounded shape of the parent, with the overall pattern emulating the Scallop Shell after which the smaller secondary rounding forms are named. As you can see from the example below, volume tends to mirror the shape of the rounding pattern in prices. Of particular note is the low or flat volume which occurs at approximately the nadir or trough of the pattern—a key element in spotting the Rounding turn around the middle of its construction.

We bring this pattern to your attention for two reasons. Currently, four Rounding Bottoms/Saucers have developed in long recommended issues. Three of these, Pennzoil, Louisiana Pacific, and Merrill Lynch, were recommended as Saucers when they were confirmed. The fourth, Firestone Tire and Rubber, was added last December on a breakout and formed a Saucer during its March to October correction. The relatively slow nature of this Reversal pattern, despite swift rallies in the above issues which confirmed their respective turns, needs to be emphasized. Should these issues turn sideways or drift lower near term, it would be in *keeping with the nature of the beast.* Option traders, therefore, should be careful about positioning in this pattern especially after the explosive confirming rally has ended; the time premium on your option could early run out before the next upleg. Our second reason for reviewing Rounding Bottoms is similar to the alert given by bird-watching groups when an in avian is spotted—*you should be looking for a bird!*

FIGURE 16

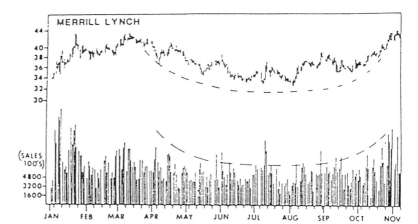

Analyzing Bar Charts for Profit

December 20, 1986

FLAGS, TRIANGLES AND RIVER SEDIMENT

What does the thickness of river sediments have to do with classic technical analysis? Quite a lot according to an interesting article in the December, 1986 issue of *Technical Analysis of Stocks and Commodities*, one of the better monthly magazines devoted to the subject. The author, Curtis McKallip, Jr., is a consultant on risk analysis in oil exploration. Mr. McKallip wrote his master thesis on the Markov transitions in river sediments of the Triassic age in East Central New Mexico (you wouldn't need a sleeping pill if you had that tome by your bed). The statistical method used to measure the shifting sediments of the river is applied to equally "shifty" transitions between stock patterns as defined by *Technical Analysis of Stock Trends* by Robert D. Edwards and John Magee.

The pattern base for the study, which was titled, *Investigating Chart Patterns Using Markov Analysis*, was weekly prices of 19 commodities from 1970-1979. Mr. McKallip marked the obvious formations on his weekly charts, using the one that was best defined when one pattern enclosed another. Complex patterns, however, were broken into component parts, i.e., the Head-and-Shoulders pattern was not measured as a unit but was considered a collection of Trends, Triangles and Flags. The article did include a long-term chart of wheat in which the various patterns were marked and identified. As a long time practitioner of pattern recognition, we had problems with some of the author's chart interpretations and nomenclature. What he calls a Symmetrical Wedge, for instance, is a Rectangle. Chartists, of course, will disagree on formations and our differences of opinion probably would not have altered Mr. McKallip's results.

Once the charts were marked up, the next step was to count the transitions from one pattern to another and use the data to set up a Markov matrix which uses Chi-Square calculations. Mr. McKallip has included in the article a two-page description of his methodology plus references (ours included).

This writer is not well-grounded in statistical probability and has almost lost his ability to add or subtract without the use of a calculator. Therefore, I won't attempt to clarify a subject which is not clear to me. However, for those of you with a mathematical frame of mind, and access to a computer, you can obtain a copy of this magazine (for $8.00) from Technical Analysis, Inc., 9131 California Avenue SW, Seattle, WA 98136. (202) 938-0570.

Without getting bogged down in the methodology, we can appreciate the results of the study. The total number of transitions tabulated in the article was 738. A number of them were too infrequent in the sample data to be of any statistical value; surprisingly, this included Rectangles (Symmetrical Wedges). There were, however, three basic pattern groups which dominated the study: Trends (we would call most of these up or down Channels); Flags (up and down); and Triangles (Symmetrical and Asymmetrical). Mr. McKallip noted that "Symmetric Triangles seem to precede Uptrends but Asymmetric Triangles preceded Downtrends more significantly." His data shows a 64% probability that an Uptrend will follow a Symmetrical Triangle, but his numbers for Asymmetrical formations seem inconclusive to us. By far, the most significant transition pairs in the study concerned Flags and Trends. Over half (54%) of the transitions identified were either moving from a Trend to a Flag or a Flag to a Trend. The results of the analysis, however, were not surprising. The probability matrix showed that an up Flag leads to a Downtrend 66% of the time while a down Flag transforms into an Uptrend 77% of the time. *In short, Flags proved under Markov analysis to be highly valuable Continuation patterns.* Interestingly, the reverse was also true. Up Flags evolved from Downtrends 37% of the time and down Flags had a 39% probability of forming from an Uptrend.

BIG BLUE—FROM BELLWETHER TO BUST!

International Business Machines has gone from a market leader to a laggard during the past year. Over the summer, while it had already slipped from its bellwether status in performance, it did, in fact, reflect the internal technical condition of the majority of issues then struggling along in a Consolidation phase (see "Taking the Market's Temperature," June 21, 1986). But our "temperature gauge" metaphor for Big Blue faltered when new lows were consistently made during the second half of 1986 while the DJIA, and the majority of the market, were holding within Consolidation boundaries. Indeed, the spark of fire which enticed us back into IBM in November has been reduced to a smolder following Wednesday's plunge through Support. The breakdown was greatly aided, we might add, by *The Wall Street Journal*'s redoubtable "Heard on the Street" column which contained, among a few distant Bullish cries, the following pearls of Bearish wisdom:

- "IBM is still a company that's not scared enough."

- "IBM's strong balance sheet is lily white and doing nobody any good."

- "Big Blue's critics now predict a horrible first quarter."

- "Even the company's most ardent admirers anticipate terrible news (for 4th quarter and year earnings)."

- "Some analysts now say net (4th quarter) earnings more likely plunged more than 40% to $2.55 a share—and perhaps fell even more."

It is no wonder a lot of Bulls stampeded out of Big Blue this week.

Looking at this issue from a long-term point of view, however, suggests that IBM may be an excellent contrarian buy. On the daily chart, a well-defined Downward-Slanting Channel has evolved since the May, 1986 high. The lower boundary of this pattern is approximately 110. The long-term monthly chart, on the other hand, shows that a much broader Upward-Slanting Channel dominated IBM from its 1974 low to the breakout of Resistance in 1983. If the upper boundary line of this long-term Channel is extended, it provides old Resistance/new Support around 110 during 1987; note the fine test of this line during the 1984 decline. For an exceptionally long-term look at IBM, we turned to the 35-year chartbook published by Securities Research (208 Newbury Street, Boston, MA 02116). A line drawn from the 1952 low through the 1981 low crosses this year at (you guessed it) 110. We initially identified long-term Support at the 1985 low of 118, and placed our stop limit at 115.

However, due to the intersection of the above Trendlines at 110, the limit in IBM is being lowered to 110 this week.

We are not fundamentalists, and, perhaps, IBM's ills are terminal. But there are clearly some very solid technical reasons to buy Big Blue during the current reaction notwithstanding the Bearish comments in Wall Street. However, for those of you who wish to wait for a Reversal, use a penetration of the Downward-Slanting Channel at 132 to enter or add.

FIGURE 17

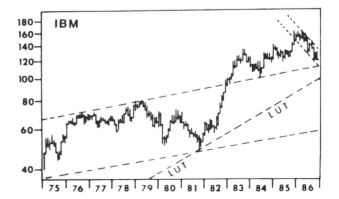

Analyzing Bar Charts for Profit

With the DJIA exploding into all-time new highs, we found this article written by John Magee nearly 25 years ago to still be a very appropriate comment on the often asked question, "How far do you think the market will go?"

THE ELUSIVE CRYSTAL BALL

A very good friend of ours, Carl Hamilton, teaches classes in technical analysis of stock trends. In the winter he teaches classes in Florida; in the summer, in New Jersey. He once wrote us concerning what he tells his students.

"I always tell them to sell at the top as they will then make so much more. When they ask me, 'What is the Top or how can one tell the Top?' I tell them, without smiling, 'When a stock does not go any higher, that is the Top.' When they ask me when do I expect the Top to be reached, I tell them, 'At exactly two o'clock this fall.'"

When somebody asks us what our "objective" is for a certain stock, or how long the rally is going to go, or whether the average is going to break 450, we are tempted to say, "Well, we're sort of handicapped right now. When Robin Davis took off for New Brunswick a couple of years ago he took our crystal ball with him; and he never sent it back. So we don't really know for sure exactly what the market is going to do in the next six months."

You could say a silly question rates a silly answer; and we think some of these questions are silly. But we realize that investors are really very seriously concerned about this market now (or for that matter the market any time); and we are not indifferent or unsympathetic. But, as we have said before, there is a good deal of nonsense talked and written about the market, and a great deal of conversation goes back and forth across the boardrooms, over the coffee tables, and around the cocktail lounges that really amounts to nothing, gets nowhere, settles no problems and means very little in terms of practical strategy and market planning.

The main reason we don't try to pin-point objectives of time or extent of a move in the market, either for a single stock or for the average, is because the forces that will determine market action may be unknown or unpredictable today. Or, isn't it better to be watching the current situation, ready to change plans in order to cope with a new development, than to be chained with a self-imposed set of predictions that have to be defended to the last ditch? There is so much talk, so many words, that often seem to express only hope or desire, not much scientific observation. Sometimes it reminds one of the prediction that "Good old Centerville High will win; or lose; or tie."

Actually, it is hard. To buy a stock on a breakout and then see it sell off on a reaction. It is hard to buy on a reaction and then sometimes see the stock go right on down to new lows. It is painful to sell short on a sharp down move which may prove to be a climax before a rally. Discouraging to wait and miss a fine opportunity altogether. These are the built-in sources of tension in the market; and the only way to handle them is to know that there are going to be disappointments, unpredictable moves, new events in the world that will call for a new look and perhaps for radically altered tactics.

In case you didn't know, we will tell you a secret. That crystal ball never did work very well. There are some good ways to operate in the market, we believe, but they don't depend on being able to "forecast the future" with absolute certainty and pin-point accuracy.

EARNINGS FORECASTS:
DANGEROUS TO YOUR FINANCIAL HEALTH!

A recent article in *Forbes*, entitled "Upward Bias," asked the question, "Is it possible that analysts concoct future earnings to justify today's lofty stock prices?" The answer appears to be yes. In a group of 20 issues, which analysts were forecasting as the fastest-growing companies two years ago, the author showed that there was a whopping (surprise) error factor of a minus 73%. This means the average earnings forecast for this group of stocks was *73% under* the actual earnings result.

This got us to thinking about a significant peril in fundamental analysis which we read about a few years back in *Contrarian Investment Strategy*, by David Dreman. Mr. Dreman, in fact, was quoted in the *Forbes* article. Because it is clothed in presumably hard data, with an air of academic certainty, fundamental research reports are often taken as "gospel." Although Mr. Dreman is not an advocate of technical analysis, for the often-cited reason that academic evidence is lacking, his comments on the pitfalls in fundamental analysis were especially cogent and important when one considers how it dominates the decision-making process in the financial industry. According to Mr. Dreman, "Research has demonstrated that earnings and dividends are the most important determinants of stock prices over time. The core of fundamental analysis is, thus, the development of techniques that will estimate these factors accurately." But, he concludes, after looking at the record, "...a system that appears eminently sensible in theory has proved *exceptionally refractory in practice*."

Without going into considerable detail in this article, we believe Mr. Dreman made a strong case for the argument that the root problem has to do with the fact that "there are very serious flaws in the analytical methods (of fundamental forecasting) that lead to consistent investment error." Briefly, the problem lies with man's information-processing capabilities. The human mind processes data in a linear manner. It moves from one point to the next in a "logical sequence." However, analyzing complex financial data requires the ability of the analysts to change the interpretation of any single piece of information depending on how he evaluates many other inputs. This is called configural reasoning and, from various tests on the subject, it appears that most of us just *cannot* do it very well.

Thus, given the complexities of determining corporate earnings, it should not be surprising that analysts and corporate management have an abysmal forecasting record. Indeed, in just one of many studies cited in the book *Financial Management's 1977 Study of Earnings Forecasts on 92 NYSE Listed Companies, From 1972-1976*, over the entire time span, the error (between the analysts' forecast and actual earnings) ran to 26.6% annually. This might seem an improvement over the *Forbes* data, but when you realize that "even a 5% or 6% miss of the forecast can unleash waves of selling," the problem with earnings projections—the foundation of fundamental analysis—and the *danger they present* to your financial health can be appreciated.

HOW FAR WILL IT GO?

One of the questions most frequently asked of our technical staff is, "How far do you think XYZ stock will go?" Although that is a good question, our usual response is to reply that we don't know. And, of course, nobody really does know ahead of time where the Top or Bottom of a stock lies. Using basic Trendlines, Support/Resistance levels and other Reaction rules, one can *estimate* pullback points reasonably well. But judging the extent of movement in the direction of the Trend is much more difficult, especially since stocks tend to advance or decline further than expected with great regularity.

There are, however, certain patterns which allow the chartist the opportunity to project at least an interim target level in the direction of the prevailing Trend. The most important of these patterns are found below:

Triangles: When a stock breaks out of a Symmetrical Triangle (either up or down), the ensuing move should carry at least as far as the height of the Triangle as measured along its first Reaction. In the illustration below, Schlumberger offers a good example of a Triangle Breakout with interim target projection. The measurement would be taken from the leg marked AB, and the objective plotted by the CD leg. Right Triangles would be measured in a similar fashion.

Rectangles: The minimum you would expect from a breakout (up or down) out of a Rectangle pattern would be the distance equal to the height of the formation (see AMAX).

Head-and-Shoulders Tops/Bottoms: The Head-and-Shoulders pattern has one of the better measuring sticks. On either a Top or Bottom the interim target, once the Neckline is penetrated, is the distance from the Top (or Bottom) of the Head to the level of the Neckline directly below (above) the Head. The American Medical Int'l chart illustrates this measurement.

Pennants and Flags: The one thing to remember about these Continuation patterns is that they "fly at half mast." In other words, the leg in equals the leg out. The Skyline chart offers a fine example of a Bull Flag.

We would remind you that measuring implications are for minimum movement following an upside or downside breakout. If a target is reached, the stock may continue on its way heedless of the measurement, or it might pause at the prescribed level and begin another pattern. But these measurements also offer the technical trader help in making the decision as to whether the situation offers enough potential gain to be worth the risks involved. It also helps in identifying areas on the chart where a Top or Bottom formation might ultimately develop.

FIGURE 18

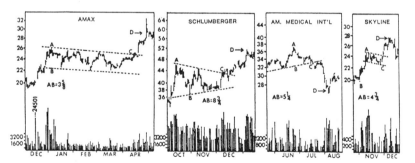

WEDGE REVIEW—A BEARISH TALE

You may have noticed that in the selling recommendations we have made over the past several weeks, the pattern which triggered the short was usually a Rising Wedge. This pattern, and its cousin the Pennant, have been the dominant formations to emerge since Black Monday. We felt, therefore, that it would be appropriate to review the Rising Wedge this week and reaquaint subscribers with the pattern's significance as well as its specific traits.

As in a Triangle, the trading activity in a Wedge oscillates within converging straight lines. Unlike the Triangle, both converging lines point in the same direction; up for a Rising Wedge and down for a Falling Wedge. The latter pattern, not in evidence at this time, has Bullish implications. But aside from breakout volume requirements, which we will discuss shortly, both patterns share similar traits.

The ascending boundary lines (see example) appear to portend higher prices and on the surface look Bullish. But unlike the Ascending Triangle, which a Rising Wedge can resemble, particularly if the upper boundary is relatively near the horizontal, there isn't a specific barrier of supply which must be overcome, and which provides a spring or significant breakout point to encourage additional demand for the stock. The advancing waves of the Rising Wedge become progressively weaker on each new high. At some point, demand *simply peters out* and the stock falls out of the pattern.

A Rising Wedge can develop as a Topping-Out pattern on an existing Uptrend. But they are more often found as temporary reactions against the Trend in a Bear Market. Indeed, during the early stage of development, Rising Wedges are usually considered to be Pennants, or Continuation patterns. Pennants, however, are generally resolved within four weeks and Rising Wedges are seldom completed in less than three weeks.

In addition to the direction of boundary lines, Rising Wedges differ from Triangles in the breakout point. The latter should exit the pattern before the three-quarter mark (from base to apex) is reached. The Rising Wedge, on the other hand, should hold within the converging boundaries for at least two-thirds of the way to the apex. In many cases, it will move into, and slightly through, the apex—a "last-gasp" rally—before turning lower. Volume during a Wedge, Rising or Falling, will be similar to a Triangle, i.e., it gradually diminishes as the stock moves into the apex of the Wedge. The breakout may or may not be accompanied by increased trading activity. A pick-up in volume is necessary to confirm an upside breakout in a Falling Wedge, *but it is not a requirement of the Rising Wedge.* Incidentally, this is common to all patterns. It takes volume to make a stock move higher, but a stock can fall on little or no volume.

Wedges are not considered to be Major patterns. They are minor formations and have, at most, only Intermediate Trend implications. The minimum objective for a Wedge is a return to the base of the pattern. Once achieved, it does not mean that the primary Downtrend is over. But a retracement of the ground within the Wedge satisfies pattern requirements and ends its effectiveness as a technical indicator. As a result, we suggest that subscribers take profits on half of their positions at Wedge objective points.

FIGURE 19

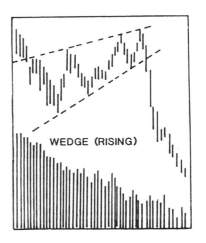

WEDGE (RISING)

Analyzing Bar Charts for Profit

IBM VERSUS DOW JONES AVERAGES

In connection with the weekly chart, (see Figure 20) we have added (on a rotational basis with *Page One* on interest rates, inflation, and currency charts) the long-term monthly chart of the DJIA. Originally, we planned to use the S&P 500 and Value Line Indices. But there is little noticeable difference between them, and we have more data on the DJIA.

Within the body of the DJIA, you will see two inset charts. The larger chart is a monthly of IBM. As we have commented in the past, an upmove in the DJIA is unlikely to hold without the participation of IBM, the largest component of the Industrial index. IBM has held within a tight 102-124 trading range since the October crash, and this shows up on the monthly chart as a Rectangle. For the current rally in the market, as measured by the DJIA to have staying power, IBM will need 93% breakout of this trading range on the upside (127) while exhibiting good volume. (Note: This week's rally fell a little short of a Confirming Breakout, but the high-volume advance does suggest the Bulls are finding Big Blue attractive once again.)

The second chart is the monthly price action from the late 1920s to early 1930s. Although there is little economic reason to equate the two periods, the pattern of trading remains remarkably similar. Until the 1988 chart begins to diverge significantly from 1939, comparisons will be inevitable. We should point out, however, that the break in 1929 decisively penetrated the long-term Uptrend Line while the 1987 version did not. From a long-term point of view, therefore, this is still a Bull Market and the current rally is potentially the next Upleg to new highs.

FIGURE 20

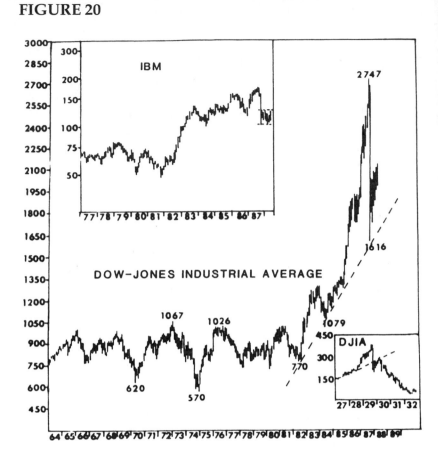

CURRENCY SWINGS

US Dollar Index—Over the past month, the Dollar, as measured by the weekly chart of the Dollar Index, broke out of a six-month-long Triangle pattern. This suggests that the three-year slide in the Dollar may be at its end. The sustained decline, however, has left a large number of significant Resistance points at former highs and lows. These levels will slow down the recovery process and may lead to more base building over the ensuing weeks. But last year's fourth-quarter low now looks like a Bottom, and we expect the general Trend in the Dollar will be higher.

Japanese Yen—The Yen broke through the Bottom of our estimated Triangle pattern, penetrating the three-year LUT and boundary line of the Up Channel in the process. The next important near-term Support point should be against last year's second-quarter high (730). A rally back into the Triangle, however, would set up the possibility that a Falling Wedge has developed over the past two quarters, implying a test of the high before a Top in the Yen can be established.

Deutsche Mark—Unlike the Yen, the Deutsche Mark has left little doubt that a Top is in place. The Dollar would need to take a significant turn for the worse to make the Deutsche Mark chart Bullish.

FIGURE 21

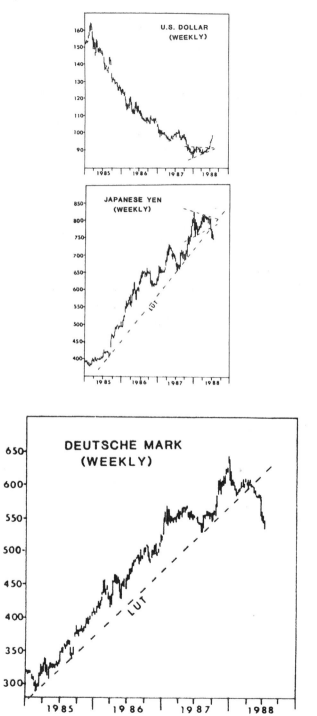

Analyzing Bar Charts for Profit

Glossary

ACCUMULATION—The first phase of a Bull Market. The period when far-sighted investors began to buy shares from discouraged or distressed sellers. Financial reports are usually at their worst and the public is completely disgusted with the stock market. Volume is only moderate, but beginning to increase on the rallies.

ACTIVITY—*See Volume.*

APEX—The highest point; the pointed end or tip of a Triangle.

ARBITRAGE—The simultaneous buying and selling of two different, but closely related, securities to take advantage of a disparity in their prices in one market or different markets.

AREA GAP—*See Common Gap.*

AREA PATTERN—When a stock or commodity's upward or downward momentum has been temporarily exhausted, the ensuing sideways movement in the price usually traces out a design or arrangement of form called an Area Pattern. The shape of some of these Area Patterns, or formations, have predictive value under certain conditions. *See Ascending Triangle, Broadening Formations, Descending Triangle, Diamond, Flag, Head-and Shoulders, Inverted Triangle, Pennant, Rectangle, Right-Angle Triangles, Symmetrical Triangles, and Wedges.*

ARITHMETIC SCALE—Price or volume scale where the distance on the vertical axis (i.e., space between horizontal lines) represents equal amounts of dollars or number of shares.

ASCENDING (PARALLEL) TREND CHANNEL—When the Tops of the rallies composing an advance develop along a line (sometimes called a return line), which is also parallel to the basic Up Trendline (i.e., the line which slopes up across the

AREA PATTERN
When a stock or commodity's upward or downward momentum has been temporarily exhausted, the ensuing sideways movement in the price usually traces out a design or arrangement of form called an Area Pattern. The shape of some of these Area Patterns, or formations, have predictive value under certain conditions.

One of a class of Area Patterns called Right-Angle Triangles. The class is distinguished by the fact that one of the two boundary lines is practically horizontal while the other slants towards it. If the top line is horizontal, and the lower slants upward to an intersection point to the right, the resulting Area Pattern is called Ascending Triangle. The implication is Bullish, with the expectant breakout though the horizontal line. Measuring formula: Add the broadest part of Triangle to the breakout point.

wave Bottoms in an advance), the area between the two lines is called an Ascending or Up Channel.

ASCENDING (UP) TRENDLINE—The advancing wave in a stock or commodity is composed of a series of ripples. When the Bottoms of these ripples form on, or very close to, an upward-slanting straight line, a basic Ascending or Up Trendline is formed.

ASCENDING TRIANGLE—One of a class of Area Patterns called Right-Angle Triangles. The class is distinguished by the fact that one of the two boundary lines is practically horizontal while the other slants towards it. If the top line is horizontal, and the lower slants upward to an intersection point to the right, the resulting Area Pattern is called Ascending Triangle. The implication is Bullish, with the expectant breakout though the horizontal line. Measuring formula: Add the broadest part of Triangle to the breakout point.

AT THE MONEY—An option the strike price of which is equal to the market value of the underlying futures contract.

AVERAGES—*See Dow-Jones Industrial Averages, Moving Averages, Dow-Jones Transportation Averages, and Dow-Jones Utility Averages.*

AVERAGING COST—An investing technique where the investor buys a stock or commodity at successively lower prices, thereby "averaging down" his average cost of each stock share or commodity contract. Purchases at successively higher prices would "average up" the price of stock shares or commodity contracts.

AXIS—In the graphical sense, an Axis is a straight line for measurement or reference. It is also the line, real or imagined, on which a formation is regarded as rotating.

BALANCED PROGRAM—Proportioning capital, or a certain part of capital, equally between the long side and the short side of the market.

BAR CHART—Also called a Line Chart. A graphic representation of prices using a vertical bar to connect the highest price in the time period to the lowest price. Opening prices are noted with a small horizontal line to the left. Closing prices are shown with a small horizontal line to the right. Bar Charts can be constructed for any time period in which prices are available. The most common time periods found in bar charts are hourly, daily, weekly and monthly. However, with the growing number of personal computers and the availability of "real time" quotes, it is not unusual for traders to use some period of minutes to construct a Bar Chart.

BASING POINT—The price level in the chart which determines where a Stop Loss Point is placed. As technical conditions change, the Basing Point, and Stops, can be advanced (in a rising market), or lowered (in a falling market). *See Progressive Stops.*

BASIC TRENDLINES—*See Trendlines.*

BASIS POINTS—The measure of yields on bonds and notes, one Basis Point equals 0.01% of yield.

BASKET TRADES—Large transactions made up of a number of various stocks.

BEAR MARKET—In its simplest form, a Bear Market is a period when prices are primarily declining; usually for a long period of time. Bear Markets generally consist of three phases: the first phase is distribution; the second is panic; and the third is akin to a washout, where those investors who have held through the first two phases, finally give up and liquidate.

BENT NECKLINE—*See Neckline.*

BETA—Higher sensitivity to market swings.

BETA (COEFFICIENT)—A measure of the market or nondiversifiable risk associated with any given security in the market.

BAR CHART
Also called a Line Chart. A graphic representation of prices using a vertical bar to connect the highest price in the time period to the lowest price. Opening prices are noted with a small horizontal line to the left. Closing prices are shown with a small horizontal line to the right. Bar Charts can be constructed for any time period in which prices are available. The most common time periods found in bar charts are hourly, daily, weekly and monthly. However, with the growing number of personal computers and the availability of "real time" quotes, it is not unusual for traders to use some period of minutes to construct a Bar Chart.

BLOCK TRADES—Large transactions of a particular stock sold as a unit.

BLOW-OFF—*See Climactic Top.*

BLUE CHIPS—The nickname given to generally high-priced companies with good records of earnings, dividends, and price stability. Also called Gilt-Edged Securities. Examples: IBM, AT&T, General Motors and General Electric.

BLUE PARALLEL—A line drawn parallel to the Trendline (Blue Trendline) which connects at least two highs. The blue parallel is started off a low and used to estimate the next low point.

BLUE TRENDLINE—A straight line connecting two or more Tops together. To avoid confusion, Edwards and Magee use a blue line for Top Trendlines and a red line for Bottom Trendlines.

BOOK VALUE—The theoretical measure of what a stock is worth based on the value of the company's assets less the company's debt.

BOTTOM—*See Ascending Triangle, Dormant Bottom, Double Bottom, Head-and-Shoulders Bottom, Rounding Bottom, and Selling Climax.*

BOUNDARY—The edges of a pattern.

BOWL—*See Rounding Bottom.*

BRACKETING—A trading range market or a price area that is non-Trending.

BREAKAWAY GAP—The hole or Gap in the chart created when a stock or commodity breaks out of an Area Pattern.

BREAKOUT—When a stock or commodity exits an Area Pattern.

BLUE PARALLEL
A line drawn parallel to the Trendline (Blue Trendline) which connects at least two highs. The blue parallel is started off a low and used to estimate the next low point.

BREAKAWAY GAP
The hole or Gap in the chart created when a stock or commodity breaks out of an Area Pattern.

Analyzing Bar Charts for Profit

BROADENING FORMATION—Sometimes called Inverted Triangles, these are formations which start with narrow fluctuations that widen out between diverging, rather than converging, boundary lines. *See also Right-Angled Broadening Formations, Broadening Top, Head-and-Shoulders and Diamond Patterns.*

BROADENING TOP—An Area Reversal pattern which may evolve in any one of three forms, comparable in shape, respectively, to Inverted Symmetrical, Ascending, or Descending Triangles. Unlike Triangles, however, the Tops and Bottoms of these patterns do not necessarily stop at clearly market-diverging boundary lines. Volume, rather than diminishing in Triangles, tends to be unusually high and irregular throughout pattern construction. No measuring formula is available.

BULL MARKET—A period when prices are primarily rising; normally for an extended period. Usually, but not always, divisible into three phases. The first phase is accumulation. The second phase is one of fairly steady advance with increasing volume. And the third phase is marked by considerable activity as the public begins to recognize and attempt to profit from the rising market.

CALL—An option that gives the buyer the right to buy the underlying contract at a specific price within a certain time period and that obligates the seller to sell the contract for the premium received before expiration of the designated time period.

CALL MARGIN—*See Margin Call.*

CALL OPTION—An option that gives the buyer the right to buy the underlying contract at a specific price within a certain period, and that obligates the seller to sell the contract for the premium received before expiration of the designated time period.

CATS AND DOGS—Low-priced stocks of questionable investment value.

CHANNEL—If the Tops of the rallies and Bottoms of the reactions develop lines which are approximately parallel to one another, the area between these lines is called a Channel. *See also Ascending Trend Channel, Descending Trend Channel, and Horizontal Trend Channel.*

CHART—A graphic representation of a stock or commodity in terms of price and/or volume. *See also Bar Chart and Point & Figure Chart.*

CLEAN-OUT DAY—*See Selling Climax.*

CLIMACTIC TOP—A sharp advance, accompanied by extraordinary volume, i.e., much larger volume than the normal increase, which signals the final "blow-off" of the Trend; followed by either a Reversal, or at least by a period of stagnation, formation of Consolidation Pattern, or a correction.

CLIMAX DAY—*See One-Day Reversal.*

CLIMAX, SELLING—*See Selling Climax.*

CLOSING PRICE—The last sale price of the trading secession for a stock. In a commodity, it represents an official price determined from a range of prices deemed to have traded at or on the close; also called a Settlement Price.

CLOSING THE GAP—When a stock or commodity returns to a previous Gap and retraces the range of the Gap. Also called Covering The Gap or Filling The Gap. *See Gap.*

COIL—Another term for a Symmetrical Triangle.

COMMISSION—The amount charged by a brokerage house to execute a trade in a stock, option, or commodity transaction. A commission is charged for each purchase and each sale. In a commodity, a commission is charged only when the original entry trade has been closed with an off-setting trade. This is called a round-turn commission.

COMMON GAP—Also called Area Gap. Any hold or Gap in the chart occurring within an Area Pattern. The forecasting significance of the Common Gap is nil. *See Gap.*

COMPARATIVE RELATIVE STRENGTH—Compares the price movement of a stock with that of its competitors, industry group or the whole market.

COMPLEX HEAD-AND-SHOULDERS—Also called Multiple Head-and-Shoulders, it is a Head-and-Shoulders pattern with more than one right and left Shoulder and/or Head. *See Head-and-Shoulders Pattern.*

COMPOSITE AVERAGE—A stock average composed of the 65 stocks which make up the Dow-Jones Industrial Average, the Dow-Jones Utility Average.

COMPOSITE LEVERAGE—In the Edwards and Magee book, *Technical Analysis of Stock Trends*, it is a formula for combining the principal factors affecting a given sum of capital used (i.e., sensitivity, price and margin) into one index figure.

CONFIRMATION—In a pattern, it is the point at which a stock or commodity exits an Area Pattern in the expected direction by an amount of price and volume sufficient to meet minimum pattern requirements for a bonafide Breakout. In the Dow Theory, it means both the Industrial Average and the Transportation Average have registered new highs or lows during the same advance or decline. If only one of the Averages establishes a new high (or low) and the other one does not, it would be a non-confirmation, or divergence. This is also true of Oscillators. To confirm a new high (or low) in a stock or commodity, an Oscillator needs to reach a new high (or low) as well. Failure of the Oscillator to confirm a new high (or low) is called a Divergence and would be considered an early indication of a potential Reversal in direction.

CONGESTION—The sideways trading from which Area Patterns evolve. Not all Congestion periods produce a recognizable pattern, however.

COMPLEX HEAD-AND-SHOULDERS
Also called Multiple Head-and-Shoulders, it is a Head-and-Shoulders pattern with more than one right and left Shoulder and/or Head.

CONGESTION
The sideways trading from which Area Patterns evolve. Not all Congestion periods produce a recognizable pattern, however.

CONSOLIDATION PATTERN—Also called a Continuation Pattern, it is an Area Pattern which breaks out in the direction of the previous Trend. *See Ascending Triangle, Descending Triangle, Flag, Head-and-Shoulders Consolidation, Pennant, Rectangle, Scallop, and Symmetrical Triangle.*

CONTINUATION GAP—*See Runaway Gap.*

CONTINUATION PATTERN—*See Consolidation Pattern.*

CONVERGENT PATTERN (TREND)—Those patterns with upper and lower boundary lines which meet, or converge, at some point if extended to the right. *See Ascending Triangle, Descending Triangle, Symmetrical Triangle, Wedges, and Pennants.*

CORRECTION—A move in a commodity or stock which is opposite to the prevailing Trend, but not sufficient to change that Trend. Called a Rally in a Downtrend and a Reaction in an Uptrend. In the Dow Theory, a correction is a Secondary Trend against the Primary Trend, which usually lasts from three weeks to three months and retraces from one-third to two-thirds of the preceding swing in the primary direction.

COVERING THE GAP—*See Closing The Gap.*

CRADLE—The intersection of the two converging boundary lines of a Symmetrical Triangle. *See Apex.*

DAILY RANGE—The difference between the high and low price during one trading day.

DEMAND—Buying interest for a stock at a given price.

DESCENDING (PARALLEL) TREND CHANNEL—When the Bottoms of the Reactions comprising a decline develop along a line (sometimes called a Return Line), which is also parallel to the basic Down Trendlines (i.e., the line which slopes down across the wave Tops in a decline), the area between the two lines is called a Descending or Down Channel.

DESCENDING TRENDLINE—The declining wave in a stock or commodity is composed of a series of ripples. When the Tops of these ripples form on, or very close to, a downward-slanting straight line, a basic Descending or Down Trendline is formed.

DESCENDING TRIANGLE—One of a class of Area Patterns called Right-Angled Triangles. The class is distinguished by the fact that one of the two boundary lines is practically horizontal while the other slants towards it. If the bottom line is horizontal and the upper slants downward to an intersection point to the right, the resulting Area Pattern is called a Descending Triangle. The implication is Bearish, with the expectant breakout through the flat (horizontal) side. Minimum measuring formula: Add the broadest part of the Triangle to the breakout point.

DIAMOND—Usually a Reversal Pattern, but it will also be found as a Continuation Pattern. It could be described as a Complex Head-and-Shoulders Pattern with a V-shaped (bent) Neckline; or a Broadening Pattern which, after two or three swings, changes into a regular Triangle. The overall shape is a four-point Diamond. Since it requires a fairly active market, it is more often found at Major Tops. Many Complex Head-and-Shoulder Tops are borderline Diamond Patterns. The major difference is in the right side of the pattern. It should clearly show two converging lines with diminishing volume as in a Symmetrical Triangle. Minimum measuring formula: Add the greatest width of the pattern to the breakout point.

DISTRIBUTION—The first phase of a Bear Market, which really begins in the last stage of a Bull Market. The period when far-sighted investors sense that the market has outrun its fundamentals, and begin to unload their holdings at an increasing pace. Trading volume is still high, however, it tends to diminish on Rallies. The public is still active but beginning to show signs of caution as hoped-for profits fade away.

DIVERGENCE—When new highs (or lows) in one indicator are not realized in another comparable indicator. *See Confirmation.*

DESCENDING TRENDLINE

The declining wave in a stock or commodity is composed of a series of ripples. When the Tops of these ripples form on, or very close to, a downward-slanting straight line, a basic Descending or Down Trendline is formed.

DIVERGENT PATTERN (TREND)—Those patterns with upper and lower boundary lines which meet at some point if extended to the left. *See Broadening Formation.*

DIVERSIFICATION—The concept of placing your funds in different industry groups and investment vehicles to spread risk. Not placing all you financial eggs in one basket.

DIVIDENDS—A share of the profits—in cash or stock equivalent—which is paid to stockholders.

DORMANT BOTTOM—A variation of a Rounding (Bowl) Bottom, but in an extended, flat-Bottomed form. It usually appears in "thin" stocks, (i.e., those issues with a small number of shares outstanding) and, characteristically, will show lengthy periods during which no sales will be registered for days at a time. The chart will appear "fly-specked" due to the missing days. The technical implication is for an Upside Breakout.

DOUBLE BOTTOM—Reversal Pattern. A Bottom formed on relatively high volume which is followed by a Rally (of at least 15%) and then a second Bottom (possibly rounded) at the same level (plus or minus 3%) as the first Bottom on lower volume. A Rally back though the Apex of the intervening Rally confirms the Reversal. More than a month should separate the two Bottoms. Minimum measuring formula: Take the distance from the lowest Bottom to the Apex of the intervening Rally and add it to the Apex.

DOUBLE TOP—A high-volume Top is formed followed by a reaction (of at least 15%) on diminishing activity. Another Rally back to the previous high (plus or minus 3%) is made, but on lower volume than the first high. A decline though the low of the reaction confirms the Reversal. The two highs should be more than a month apart. Minimum measuring formula: Add to the breakout point the distance from the highest peak to the low of the Reaction. Also called an "M" Formation.

DORMANT BOTTOM

A variation of a Rounding (Bowl) Bottom, but in an extended, flat-Bottomed form. It usually appears in "thin" stocks, (i.e., those issues with a small number of shares outstanding) and, characteristically, will show lengthy periods during which no sales will be registered for days at a time. The chart will appear "fly-specked" due to the missing days. The technical implication is for an Upside Breakout.

DOUBLE TRENDLINE—When two relatively close parallel Trendlines are needed to define the true Trend pattern. *See Trendline.*

DOW-JONES INDUSTRIAL AVERAGE—Developed by Charles Dow in 1885 to study market trends. Originally composed of 14 companies (12 railroads and 2 industrials), the rails by 1897 were separated into their own average, and 12 industrial companies of the day were selected for the industrial average. The number was increased to 20 in 1916 and to 30 in 1928. The stocks included in this average have been changed from time to time to keep the list up to date, or to accommodate a merger. The only original issue still in the average is General Electric.

DOW-JONES TRANSPORTATION AVERAGE—Established at the turn of the century with the new Industrial Average, it was originally called the Rail Average and composed of 20 railroad companies. With the advent of the airlines industry, the average was updated in 1970 and the name changed to Transportation Average.

DOW-JONES UTILITY AVERAGE—In 1929, utility companies were dropped from the Industrial Average and a new Utility Average of 20 companies was created. In 1938, the number of issues was reduced to the present 15.

DOWNTICK—A securities transaction which is at a price that is lower than the preceding transaction.

DOWNTREND—*See Descending Trendline and Trend.*

END RUN—When a breakout of a Symmetrical Triangle pattern reverses its direction and trades back through Axis Support (if an Upside Breakout) or Resistance (if a Downside Breakout), it is termed an End Run around the line, or End Run for short. The term is sometimes used to denote Breakout failure in general.

EQUILIBRIUM MARKET—A price area that represents a balance between demand and supply.

EX-DIVIDEND—The day when the dividend is subtracted from the price of the stock.

EX-DIVIDEND GAP—The Gap in price caused when the price of a stock is adjusted downward after the dividend payment is deducted.

EXERCISE—The means by which the holder of an option purchases or sells shares of the underlying security.

EXHAUSTION GAP—Relatively wide Gap in the price of a stock or commodity which occurs near the end of a strong directional move in the price. These Gaps are quickly closed, most often within two to five days, which helps to distinguish them from Runaway Gaps which are not usually covered for a considerable length of time. An Exhaustion Gap cannot be read as a Major Reversal, or even necessarily a Reversal. It signals a halt in the prevailing Trend which is ordinarily followed by some sort of Area Pattern development.

EXPIRATION—The last day on which an option can be exercised.

EXPOTENTIAL SMOOTHING—A mathematical-statistical methodology of forecasting that assumes future price action is a weighted average of past periods; a mathematic series in which greater weight is given to more recent price action.

FALLING WEDGE—An Area Pattern with two downward-slanting, converging Trendlines. Normally it takes more than three weeks to complete, and volume will diminish as prices move toward the Apex of the pattern. The anticipated direction of the Breakout in a Falling Wedge is up. Minimum measuring formula: A Retracement of all the ground lost within the Wedge. *See Wedge.*

FALSE BREAKOUT—A breakout which is confirmed but which quickly reverses and eventually leads the stock or commodity to a Breakout in the opposite direction. Indistinguishable from Premature Breakout or Genuine Breakout when it occurs.

FAN LINES—A set of three Secondary Trendlines drawn from the same starting high or low, which spread out in a fan shape. In a primary Uptrend, the Fan would be along the Tops of the Secondary (Intermediate) Reaction. In a Primary Downtrend, the Fan would be along the Bottoms of the Secondary (Intermediate) Rally. When the third Fan Line is broken, it signals the resumption of the Primary Trend.

50-DAY MOVING-AVERAGE LINE—Is determined by taking the closing price over the past 50 trading days and dividing by 50.

FIVE-POINT REVERSAL—*See Broadening Pattern.*

FLAG—A Continuation Pattern. A Flag is a period of Congestion, less than four weeks in duration, which forms after a sharp, near vertical, change in price. The upper and lower boundary lines of the pattern are parallel, though both may slant up, down or sideways. In an Uptrend, the pattern resembles a Flag flying from a mast, hence the name. Flags are also called Measuring or Half-Mast Patterns because they tend to form at the mid-point of the Rally or Reaction. Volume tends to diminish during the formation and increase on the Breakout. Minimum measuring formula: Add the distance from the Breakout point, which started the preceding "mast" Rally or Reaction, to the Breakout point of the Flag.

FLOATING SUPPLY—The number of shares available for trading at any given time. Generally the outstanding number of shares, less shares closely held and likely to be unavailable to the public. Shares of a company held by its employee pension fund, for example, would not generally enter the trading stream and could be subtracted from the outstanding shares.

FORMATION—*See Area Pattern.*

FRONT-MONTH—The first expiration month in a series of months.

FAN LINES
A set of three Secondary Trendlines drawn from the same starting high or low, which spread out in a fan shape. In a primary Uptrend, the Fan would be along the Tops of the Secondary (Intermediate) Reaction. In a Primary Downtrend, the Fan would be along the Bottoms of the Secondary (Intermediate) Rally. When the third Fan Line is broken, it signals the resumption of the Primary Trend.

FUNDAMENTALS—Information on a stock pertaining to the business of the company and how it relates to earnings and dividends. In a commodity, it would be information on any factor that would affect Supply or Demand.

GAP—A hole in the price range which occurs when either (1) the lowest price at which a stock or commodity is traded during any time period is higher than the highest price at which it was traded on the preceding time period, or (2) the highest prices of one time period is lower than the lowest price of the preceding time period. When the ranges of the two time periods are plotted, they will not overlap or touch the same horizontal level on the chart—there will be a price Gap between them. *See Common or Area Gap, Ex-Dividend Gap, Breakaway Gap, Runaway Gap, Exhaustion Gap and Island Reversal.*

GRAPH—*See Chart.*

HALF-MAST FORMATION—*See Flag.*

HEAD-AND-SHOULDERS PATTERN—Although occasionally an Inverted Head-and-Shoulders Pattern (called a Consolidation Head-and-Shoulders) will form which is a Continuation Pattern. In its normal form, this pattern is one of the more common and more reliable of the Major Reversal Patterns. It consists of the following four elements (a Head-and-Shoulders Top will be described for illustration): (1) A rally which ends a more or less extensive advance on heavy volume, and which is then followed by a Minor Reaction on less volume. This is the left Shoulder; (2) Another high-volume advance which exceeds the high of the left Shoulder, followed by another low-volume Reaction which takes prices down to near the Bottom of the preceding Reaction, and below the Top of the left Shoulder high. This is the Head; (3) A third Rally, but on decidedly less volume than accompanied either of the first two advances, and which fails to exceed the high established on the Head. This is the right Shoulder; and (4) A decline through a line drawn across the preceding two reaction lows (the Neckline), and a close below that line equivalent to 3% of the stock's market price. This is the Confirmation of the Breakout. A Head-and-Shoulders Bottom, or any other combination Head-

---

> ## GAP
> *A hole in the price range which occurs when either (1) the lowest price at which a stock or commodity is traded during any time period is higher than the highest price at which it was traded on the preceding time period, or (2) the highest prices of one time period is lower than the lowest price of the preceding time period. When the ranges of the two time periods are plotted, they will not overlap or touch the same horizontal level on the chart—there will be a price Gap between them.*

and-Shoulders Pattern, contains the same four elements. The main difference between a Top formation and a Bottom formation is in the volume patterns. The Breakout in a Top can be on low volume. The Breakout in a Bottom must show a "conspicuous burst of activity." Minimum measuring formula: Add the distance between the Head and Neckline to the Breakout point.

HEAD-AND-SHOULDERS BOTTOM—Area Pattern which reverses a decline. *See Head-and-Shoulders Pattern.*

HEAD-AND-SHOULDERS CONSOLIDATION—Area Pattern which continues the previous Trend. *See Head-and-Shoulders Pattern.*

HEAD-AND-SHOULDERS TOP—Area Pattern which reverses an advance. *See Head-and-Shoulders Pattern.*

HEAVY VOLUME—The expression "heavy volume" as used by Edwards and Magee, means heavy only with respect to the recent volume of sales in the stock you are watching.

HEDGING—To try to lessen risk by making a counterbalancing investment. In a stock portfolio, an example of a Hedge would be to buy 100 shares of XYZ stock, and to buy one Put Option of the same stock. The Put would help protect against a decline in the stock, but it would also limit potential gains on the upside.

HISTORICAL DATA—A series of past daily, weekly, or monthly market prices.

HOOK DAY—A trading day in which the open is above/below prior day's high/low and the close is below/above prior day's close with narrow range.

HORIZONTAL CHANNEL—When the Tops of the Rallies and Bottoms of the Reactions form along lines which are horizontal and parallel to one another, the area in between is called a Horizontal Trend Channel. It may also be called a Rectangle during the early stages of formation.

HEAVY VOLUME
The expression "heavy volume" as used by Edwards and Magee, means heavy only with respect to the recent volume of sales in the stock you are watching.

HORIZONTAL TRENDLINE—A horizontal line drawn across either the Tops or Bottoms in a Sideways Trending market.

HYBRID HEAD-AND-SHOULDERS—A small Head-and-Shoulders Pattern within a larger Head-and-Shoulders Pattern. *See Head-and-Shoulders Pattern.*

INDUSTRIAL AVERAGE—*See Dow-Jones Industrial Average.*

INSIDE DAY—A day in which the daily price range is totally within the prior day's daily price range.

INSIDERS—Individuals who possess fundamental information likely to affect the price of a stock, but which is unavailable to the public. An example would be an individual who knows about a merger before it is announced to the public. Trading by insiders on this type of information is illegal.

INTERMEDIATE TREND—In the Edwards and Magee book, *Technical Analysis of Stock Trends*, the term Intermediate or Secondary refers to a Trend (or pattern indicating a Trend) against the Primary (Major) Trend which is likely to last from three weeks to three months, and which may retrace one-third to two-thirds of the previous primary advance or decline.

INVERTED BOWL—*See Rounding Top.*

INVERTED TRIANGLE—*See Right-Angled Broadening Triangle.*

ISLAND REVERSAL—A compact trading range, usually formed after a fast Rally or Reaction, which is separated from the previous move by an Exhaustion Gap, and from the move in the opposite direction which follows by a Breakaway Gap. The result is an island of prices detached by a Gap before and after. If the trading range contains only one day, it is called a One-Day Reversal. The two Gaps usually occur at approximately the same level. By itself, the pattern is not of major significance; but it does frequently send prices back for a complete Retracement of the Minor move which preceded it.

LEVERAGE—Using a smaller amount of capital to control an investment of greater value. For example, exclusive of interest and commission costs, if you buy a stock on 50% margin, you control $1 of stock for every 50 cents invested or Leverage of 2-to-1.

LIMIT MOVE—A change in price which exceeds the limits set by the exchange on which the contract is traded.

LIMIT ORDER—A Buy or Sell Order which is limited in some way, usually in price. For example, if you placed a Limit Order to buy IBM at 100, the broker would not fill the order unless he could do so at your price or better, i.e., at 100 or lower.

LIMIT UP, LIMIT DOWN—Commodity exchange restrictions on the maximum upward or downward movements permitted in the price for a commodity during any trading session day.

LINE, DOW THEORY—A line in the Dow Theory is an intermediate sideways movement in one or both of the Averages (industrial and/or transportation) in the course of which prices fluctuate within a range of 5% (of mean price) or less.

LOGARITHMIC SCALE—*See Semi-Logarithmic Scale.*

MAJOR TREND—In the Edwards and Magee book, *Technical Analysis of Stock Trends*, the term Major (or Primary) refers to a Trend (or pattern leading to such a Trend) which lasts at least one year, and shows a rise or decline of at least 20%.

MARGIN—The minimum amount of capital required to buy or sell a stock. The rate, currently 50% of value, is set by the government. In a commodity, margin is also the minimum, usually about 10%, needed to buy or sell a contract. But the rate is set by the individual exchanges. The two differ in cost as well. In a stock, the broker lends the investor the balance of the

LIMIT ORDER
A Buy or Sell Order which is limited in some way, usually in price. For example, if you placed a Limit Order to buy IBM at 100, the broker would not fill the order unless he could do so at your price or better, i.e., at 100 or lower.

MAJOR TREND
In the Edwards and Magee book, Technical Analysis of Stock Trends, the term Major (or Primary) refers to a Trend (or pattern leading to such a Trend) which lasts at least one year, and shows a rise or decline of at least 20%.

money due and charges interest for the loan. In a commodity, margin is treated as a good faith payment. The broker does not lend the difference so no interest expense is incurred.

MARKET ON CLOSE—An order specification which requires the broker to get the best price available on the close of trading.

MARKET ORDER—An instruction to buy or sell at the price prevailing when the order reaches the floor of the Exchange.

MARKET RECIPROCAL—Normal average range of a stock based on the average range for a number of years, divided by the current average range. The result is the reciprocal of the market movement for the period. Wide market activity, for example, would show a small decimal, less than 1. Dull trading would be a larger number.

MAST—The vertical Rally or Reaction preceding a Flag or Pennant formation.

MEASURING FORMULA—The formula for determining the minimum amount a stock or commodity is likely to move after a successful Breakout of an Area Pattern. *See individual patterns for specific formulas.*

MEASURING GAP—*See Runaway Gap.*

MINOR TREND—In the Edwards and Magee book, *Technical Analysis of Stock Trends*, the term Minor refers to brief fluctuations (usually less than six days and rarely longer than three weeks) which, in total, make up the Intermediate Trend.

MOMENTUM INDICATOR—A market indicator which utilizes volume statistics for predicting the strength or weakness of a current market and any overbought or oversold conditions, and to distinguish turning points within the market.

MOVING AVERAGE—A mathematical technique to smooth data. It is called moving because the number of elements are fixed, but the time interval advances. Old data must be removed when new data is added which causes the average to "move along" with the progression of the stock or commodity.

MOVING AVERAGE CROSSOVERS—The point where the various Moving Average Lines pass through or over each other.

MULTIPLE HEAD-AND-SHOULDERS PATTERN—*See Complex Head-and-Shoulders.*

NARROW RANGE DAY—A trading day with a narrower price range relative to the previous day's price range.

NECKLINE—In a Head-and-Shoulders Pattern, it is the line drawn across the two reaction lows (in a Top), or two rally highs (in a Bottom), which occur before and after the Head. This line must be broken by 3% to confirm the Reversal. In a Diamond Pattern, which is similar to a Head-and-Shoulders Pattern, the Neckline is bent in the shape of a V or inverted V. *See Diamond Pattern and Head-and-Shoulders Pattern.*

NEGATIVE DIVERGENCE—When two or more averages, indices or indicators fail to show confirming Trends.

ODD LOT—A block of stock consisting of less than 100 shares.

ONE-DAY REVERSAL—*See Island Reversal.*

OPTION—The right granted to one investor by another to buy (called a Call Option) or sell (called a Put Option) 100 shares of stock, or one contract of a commodity, at a fixed price for a fixed period of time. The investor granting the right (the seller of the Option) is paid a non-refundable premium by the buyer of the Option.

ORDER—*See Limit Order, Market Order, and Stop Order.*

NECKLINE
In a Head-and-Shoulders Pattern, it is the line drawn across the two reaction lows (in a Top), or two rally highs (in a Bottom), which occur before and after the Head. This line must be broken by 3% to confirm the Reversal. In a Diamond Pattern, which is similar to a Head-and-Shoulders Pattern, the Neckline is bent in the shape of a V or inverted V.

POINT & FIGURE CHART

A method of charting believed to have been created by Charles Dow. Each day the price moves by a specific amount (the arbitrary box size) an X (if up) or O (if down) is placed on a vertical column of squared paper. As long as prices do not change direction by a specified amount (the Reversal), the Trend is considered to be in force and no new column is made. If a Reversal takes place, another vertical column is started immediately to the right of the first, but in the opposite direction. There is no provision for time on a Point & Figure Chart.

OSCILLATOR—A form of momentum or rate-of-change indicator which is usually valued from +1 to -1 or from 0% to 100%.

OVERBOUGHT—Market prices that have risen too steeply and too quickly.

OVERSOLD—Market prices that have declined too steeply and too quickly.

OVERBOUGHT/OVERSOLD INDICATOR—An indicator that attempts to define when prices have moved too far and too quickly in either direction and thus are liable to a Reaction.

PANIC—The second stage of a Bear Market when buyers thin out and sellers become more urgent. The Downward Trend of prices suddenly accelerates into an almost vertical drop while volume rises to climactic proportions. *See Bear Market.*

PANIC BOTTOM—*See Selling Climax.*

PATTERN—*See Area Pattern.*

PEAK—*See Top.*

PENETRATION—The breaking of a pattern boundary line, Trendline or Support and Resistance level.

PENNANT—A Pennant is a Flag with converging, rather than parallel, boundary lines. *See Flag.*

POINT & FIGURE CHART—A method of charting believed to have been created by Charles Dow. Each day the price moves by a specific amount (the arbitrary box size) an X (if up) or O (if down) is placed on a vertical column of squared paper. As long as prices do not change direction by a specified amount (the Reversal), the Trend is considered to be in force and no new column is made. If a Reversal takes place, another vertical column is started immediately to the right of the first, but in the opposite direction. There is no provision for time on a Point & Figure Chart.

PREMATURE BREAKOUT—A Breakout of an Area Pattern, then a retreat back into the pattern. Eventually the Trend will Breakout again and proceed in the same direction. At the time they occur, False Breakout and Premature Breakouts are indistinguishable from each other, or a Genuine Breakout.

PRIMARY TREND—*See Major Trend.*

PROGRAM TRADING—Trades based on signals from various computer programs, usually entered directly from the trader's computer to the market's computer system.

PROGRESSIVE STOP—A Stop Order which follows the market up or down. *See Stop.*

PROTECTIVE STOP—A Stop Order used to protect gains or limit losses in an existing position. *See Stop.*

PULLBACK—Return of prices to the boundary line of the pattern after a Breakout to the Downside. Return after an Upside Breakout is called a Throwback.

PUT—An Option to sell a specified amount of a stock or commodity at an agreed time at the stated exercise price.

RAIL AVERAGE—*See Dow-Jones Transportation Average.*

RALLY—An increase in price which retraces part of the previous price decline.

RALLY TOPS—A price level that finishes a short-term Rally in an ongoing Trend.

RANGE—The difference between the high and low during a specific time period.

REACTION—A decline in price which retraces part of the previous price advance.

PULLBACK
Return of prices to the boundary line of the pattern after a Breakout to the Downside. Return after an Upside Breakout is called a Throwback.

RALLY
An increase in price which retraces part of the previous price decline.

REACTION
A decline in price which retraces part of the previous price advance.

RECIPROCAL, MARKET—*See Market Reciprocal.*

RECOVERY—*See Rally.*

RECTANGLE—A trading area which is bounded on the Top and the Bottom with horizontal, or near horizontal, lines. A Rectangle can be either a Reversal or Continuation Pattern depending on the direction of the Breakout. Minimum measuring formula: Add the width (difference between Top and Bottom) of the Rectangle to the Breakout point.

RED PARALLEL—A line drawn parallel to the Trendline (Red Trendline) which connects at least two Bottoms. The Red Parallel (basically a Return Line) is started off a high and used to estimate the next high point.

RED TRENDLINE—A straight line connecting two or more Bottoms together. To avoid confusion, Edwards and Magee use a red line for Bottom Trendlines and a blue line for Top Trendlines.

RESISTANCE LEVEL

A price level at which a sufficient supply of stock is forthcoming to stop, and possibly turn back for a time, an Uptrend.

RESISTANCE LEVEL—A price level at which a sufficient supply of stock is forthcoming to stop, and possibly turn back for a time, an Uptrend.

RETRACEMENT—A price movement in the opposite direction of the previous Trend.

RETURN LINE—*See Ascending or Descending Trend Channels.*

REVERSAL GAP

A chart formation where the low of the last day is above the previous day's range with the close above mid-range and above the open.

REVERSAL GAP—A chart formation where the low of the last day is above the previous day's range with the close above mid-range and above the open.

REVERSAL PATTERN—An Area Pattern which breaks out in a direction opposite to the previous Trend. *See Ascending Triangle, Broadening Formation, Broadening Top, Descending Triangle, Diamond, Dormant Bottom, Double Bottom or Top, Triple Bottom or Top, Head-and-Shoulders, Rectangle, Rounding Bottom or Top, Saucer, Symmetrical Triangle and Rising or Falling Wedge.*

RIGHT-ANGLED BROADENING TRIANGLE—Area Pattern with one boundary line horizontal and the other at an angle which, when extended, will converge with the horizontal line at some point to the left of the pattern. Similar in shape to Ascending and Descending Triangles except they are inverted and look like Flat-Topped or Bottomed megaphones. Right-Angled Broadening formations generally carry Bearish implications regardless of which side is flat. But any decisive Breakout (3% or more) through the horizontal boundary line has the same forceful significance as does a Breakout in an Ascending or Descending Triangle.

RIGHT-ANGLED TRIANGLES—*See Ascending and Descending Triangles.*

RISING WEDGE—An Area Pattern with two upward-slanting, converging Trendlines. Normally it takes more than three weeks to complete, and volume will diminish as prices move toward the Apex of the pattern. The anticipated direction of the Breakout in a Rising Wedge is down. Minimum measuring formula: A retracement of all the ground gained within the Wedge.

ROUND LOT—A block of stock consisting of 100 shares of stock.

ROUND TRIP—The cost of one complete stock or commodity transaction, i.e., the entry cost and the offset cost combined.

ROUNDING BOTTOM—An Area Pattern which pictures a gradual, progressive and fairly symmetrical change in the Trend from down to up. Both the price pattern (along its lows) and the volume pattern show a concave shape often called a Bowl or Saucer. There is no minimum measuring formula associated with this Reversal Pattern.

ROUNDING TOP—An Area Pattern which pictures a gradual, progressive and fairly symmetrical change in the Trend from up to down. The price pattern, along its highs, shows a convex shape sometime called an Inverted Bowl. The volume pattern is concave shaped (a Bowl) as trading activity declines into the peak of the price pattern, and increases when prices begin to fall. There is no measuring formula associated with this Reversal Pattern.

RUNAWAY GAP—A relatively wide Gap in prices which occurs in an advance or decline gathering momentum. Also called a "Measuring Gap" since it frequently occurs at just about the halfway point between the Breakout which started the move and the Reversal day which calls an end to it. Minimum measuring formula: Take the distance from the original Breakout point to the start of the Gap, and add it to the other side of the Gap.

RUNNING MARKET—A market wherein prices are moving rapidly in one direction with very few or no price changes in the opposite direction.

SAUCER—*See Rounding Bottom and Scallops.*

SCALLOPS—A series of Rounding Bottom (Saucers) Patterns where the rising end always carries prices a little higher than the preceding Top at the beginning of the pattern. Net gains will vary from stock to stock, but there is a strong tendency for it to amount to 10%–15% of the price. The total reaction, from the left-hand Top of each Saucer to its Bottom, is usually in the 20%–30% area. Individual Saucers in a Scallop series are normally five- to seven-weeks long and rarely less than three weeks. The volume will show a Convex or Bowl Pattern.

SECONDARY TREND—*See Intermediate Trend.*

SELLING CLIMAX—A period of extraordinary volume which comes at the end of a rapid and comprehensive decline which exhausts the margin reserves of many speculators and patience of investors. Total volume turnover may exceed any single day's volume during the previous upswing as panic selling sweeps through the stock or commodity. Also called a Clean-Out Day, a Selling Climax reverses the technical condi-

---

RUNAWAY GAP

A relatively wide Gap in prices which occurs in an advance or decline gathering momentum. Also called a "Measuring Gap" since it frequently occurs at just about the halfway point between the Breakout which started the move and the Reversal day which calls an end to it. Minimum measuring formula: Take the distance from the original Breakout point to the start of the Gap, and add it to the other side of the Gap.

tions of the market. Although it is a form of a One-Day Reversal, it can take more than one day to complete.

SEMI-LOGARITHMIC SCALE—Price or volume scale where the distance on the vertical axis (i.e., space between horizontal lines) represents equal percentage changes.

SENSITIVITY—An index used by Edwards and Magee to measure the probable percentage movement (sensitivity) of a stock during a specified percentage move in the stock market as a whole.

SHAKE-OUT—A corrective move large enough to "shake out" nervous investors before the Primary Trend resumes.

SHORT INTEREST—The number of shares that have been sold short and not yet repurchased. This information is published monthly by the New York Stock Exchange.

SHORT SALE—A transaction where the entry position is to sell a stock or commodity first and to repurchase it (hopefully at a lower price) at a later date. In the stock market, shares you do not own can be sold by borrowing shares from the broker, and replacing them when the offsetting repurchase takes place. In the commodity market, contracts are created when a buyer and seller get together through a floor broker. As a result, the procedure to sell in the commodity market is the same as it is to buy.

SHOULDER—*See Head-and-Shoulders Patterns.*

SMOOTHING—A mathematical approach that removes excess data variability while maintaining a correct appraisal of the underlying Trend.

SPIKE—A sharp rise in price in a single day or two.

STOCHASTIC—Literally means random.

STOCK SPLIT—A procedure used by management to establish a different market price for its shares by changing the

SEMI-LOGARITHMIC SCALE
Price or volume scale where the distance on the vertical axis (i.e., space between horizontal lines) represents equal percentage changes.

SMOOTHING
A mathematical approach that removes excess data variability while maintaining a correct appraisal of the underlying Trend.

common stock structure of the company. Usually a lower price is desired and established by cancelling the outstanding shares and reissuing a larger number of new certificates to current shareholders. The most common ratios are 2-to-1, 3-to-1 and 3-to-2. Occasionally, a higher price is desired and a reverse split takes place where one new share is issued for some multiple number of old shares.

STOP—A Contingency Order which is placed above the current market price if it is to buy, or below the current market price if it is to sell. A Stop Order becomes a Market Order only when the stock or commodity moves up to the price of the Buy Stop, or down to the price of a Sell Stop. A Stop can be used to enter a new position or exit an old position. *See Protective Stop or Progressive Stop.*

STOP LOSS—*See Protective Stop.*

SUPPLY—Amount of stock available at a given price.

SUPPLY LINE—*See Resistance.*

SUPPORT LEVEL—The price level at which a sufficient amount of demand is forthcoming to stop, and possibly turn higher for a time, a Downtrend.

SYMMETRICAL TRIANGLE—Also called a Coil. Can be a Reversal or Continuation Pattern. A Sideways Congestion where each Minor Top fails to attain the height of the previous Rally and each Minor Bottoms topping above the level of the previous low. The result is upper and lower boundary lines which converge, if extended, to a point on the right. The upper boundary line must slant down and the lower boundary line must slant up, or it would be a variety of Wedge. Volume tends to diminish during formation. Minimum formula: Add the widest distance within the Triangle to its Breakout point.

TANGENT—*See Trendline.*

TAPE READER—One who makes trading decisions by watching the flow of New York Stock Exchange and American

SUPPORT LEVEL
The price level at which a sufficient amount of demand is forthcoming to stop, and possibly turn higher for a time, a Downtrend.

Analyzing Bar Charts for Profit

Stock Exchange price and volume data coming across the electronic ticker tape.

TEKNIPLAT PAPER—A specially formatted two-cycle, semi-logarithmic graph paper, with sixth-line vertical accents, used to chart stock or commodity prices. (TEKNIPLAT Paper is available from John Magee, Inc.)

TEST—A term used to describe the activity of a stock or commodity when it returns to, "tests", the validity of a previous Trendline, or Support or Resistance level.

THREE-DAY AWAY RULE—An arbitrary time period used by Edwards and Magee in marking suspected Minor Tops or Bottoms.

THIN ISSUE—A stock which has a low number of floating shares and is lightly traded.

THROWBACK—Return of prices to the boundary line of the pattern after a Breakout to the Upside. Return after a Downside Breakout is called a Pullback.

TOP—*See Broadening Top, Descending Triangle, Double Top, Head-and-Shoulders Top, Triple Top and Rounding Top.*

TREND—The direction prices are moving. *See Ascending, Descending and Horizontal Parallel Trend Channels, Convergent Trend, Divergent Trend, Intermediate Trend, Major Trend and Minor Trend.*

TREND CHANNEL—A parallel probable price range centered about the most likely price line.

TRENDING MARKET—Price moves in a single direction, usually closing at an extreme for the day.

TRENDLINE—A straight line which connects a series of higher lows (an Up Trendline), a series of lower highs (a Down Trendline), or a series of highs and/or lows on a horizontal line.

VALIDITY OF TRENDLINE PENETRATION

The application of the following three tests when a Trendline is broken to determine whether the break is valid, or whether the Trendline is still basically intact: (1) The extent of the penetration, (2) The volume of trading on the penetration, and (3) The trading action after the penetration.

TRIANGLE—*See Ascending Triangle, Descending Triangle, Right Angled Broadening Triangle, and Symmetrical Triangle.*

TRIPLE BOTTOM—Similar to a Flat Head-and-Shoulders Bottom, or Rectangle, the three Bottoms in a Triple Bottom.

TRIPLE TOP—An Area Pattern with three Tops which are widely spaced and with quite deep, and usually rounding, Reactions between them. Less volume occurs on the second peak than the first peak, and still less on the third peak. Sometimes called a "W" Pattern, particularly if the second peak is below the first and third. The Triple Top is confirmed when the decline from the third Top penetrates the Bottom of the lowest valley between the three peaks.

200-DAY MOVING-AVERAGE LINE—Is determined by taking the closing price over the past 200 trading days and dividing by 200.

U/D VOLUME—Is the ratio between the daily up volume to the daily down volume. It is a fifty-day ratio which is determined by dividing the total volume on those days when the stock closed up from the prior day by the total volume on days when the stock closed down.

UPTICK—A securities transaction which is made at a price higher than the preceding transaction.

UPTREND—*See Ascending Trendline and Trend.*

UTILITY AVERAGE—*See Dow-Jones Utility Average.*

VALIDITY OF TRENDLINE PENETRATION—The application of the following three tests when a Trendline is broken to determine whether the break is valid, or whether the Trendline is still basically intact: (1) The extent of the penetration, (2) The volume of trading on the penetration, and (3) The trading action after the penetration.

VALLEY—The V-shaped price action which occurs between two peaks. *See Double Top and Triple Top.*

VOLATILITY—A measure of a stock's tendency to move up and down in price, based on its daily price history over the latest 12-month period.

VOLUME—The number of shares in stocks or contracts in commodities which are traded over a specified period of time.

"W" FORMATION—*See Triple Top.*

WEDGE—A chart formation in which the price fluctuations are confined within converging straight (or practically straight) lines, but differing from a Triangle in that both boundary lines either slope up or slope down. *See Falling Wedge and Rising Wedge.*

> **WEDGE**
> *A chart formation in which the price fluctuations are confined within converging straight (or practically straight) lines, but differing from a Triangle in that both boundary lines either slope up or slope down.*

Glossary of Patterns

This section contains chart patterns for the following:

- ■ Major Bullish (Bottoming) Patterns
- ■ Major Bearish (Topping) Patterns
- ■ Indeterminant Patterns
- ■ Major Continuation Patterns (of Previous Trend)
- ■ Measurement Patterns

MAJOR BULLISH (BOTTOMING) PATTERNS

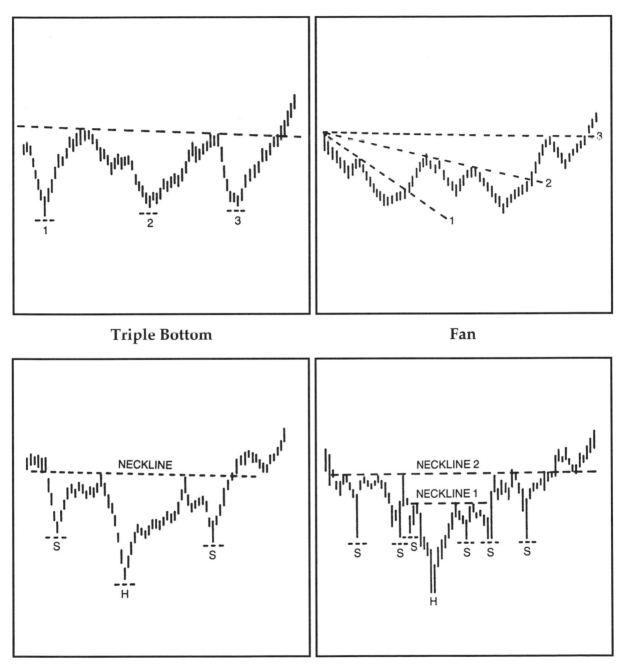

Triple Bottom

Fan

Head-and-Shoulders Bottom (Simple)

Head-and-Shoulders Bottom (Complex)

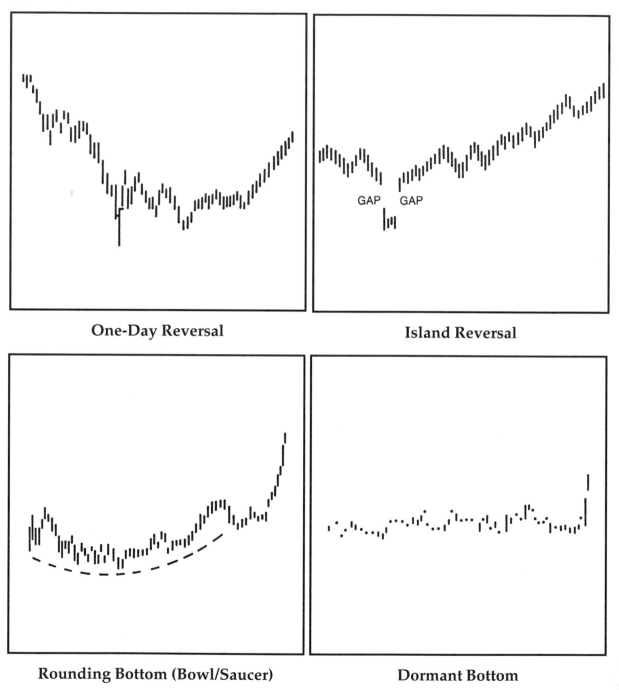

One-Day Reversal

Island Reversal

Rounding Bottom (Bowl/Saucer)

Dormant Bottom

MAJOR BEARISH (TOPPING) PATTERNS

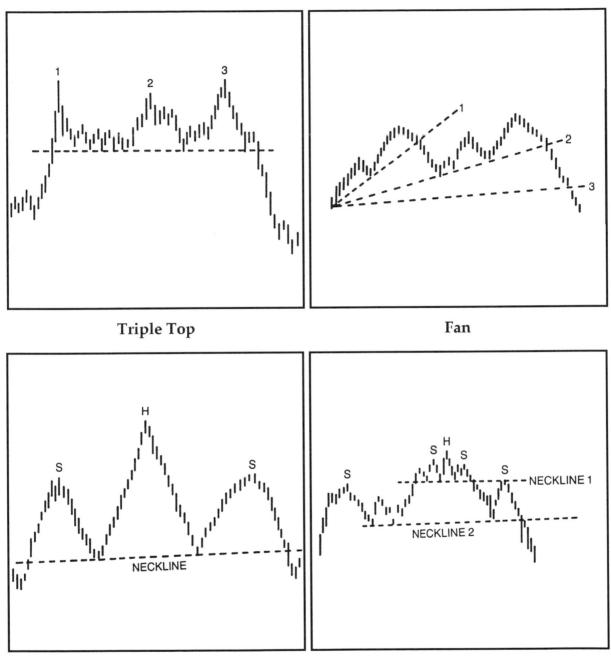

Triple Top

Fan

Head-and-Shoulders Top (Simple)

Head-and-Shoulders Top (Complex)

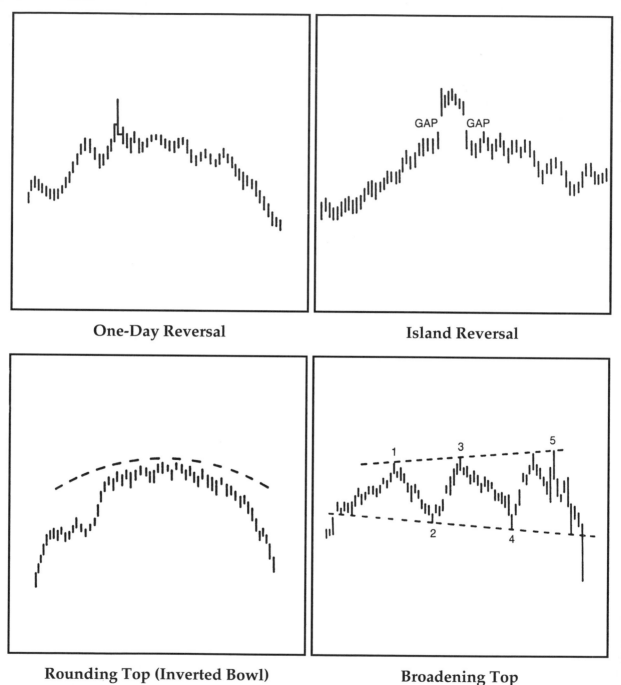

One-Day Reversal

Island Reversal

Rounding Top (Inverted Bowl)

Broadening Top

Analyzing Bar Charts for Profit

INDETERMINANT PATTERNS

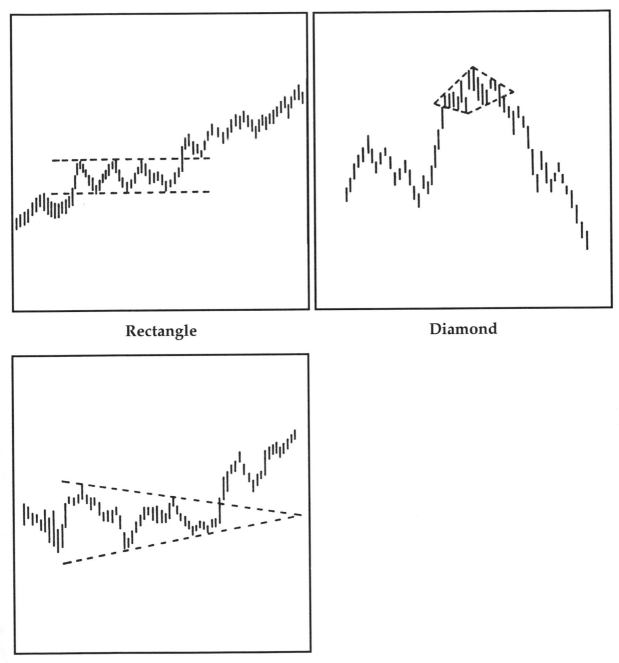

Rectangle

Diamond

Triangle (Symmetrical)

MAJOR CONTINUATION PATTERNS (OF PREVIOUS TREND)

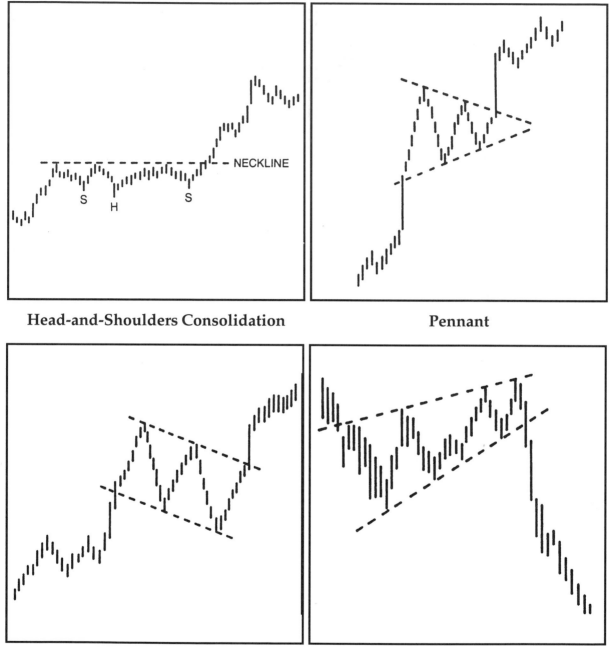

Head-and-Shoulders Consolidation

Pennant

Flag

Wedge (Rising)

Analyzing Bar Charts for Profit

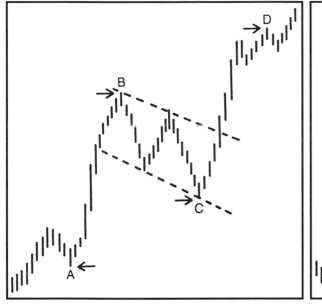

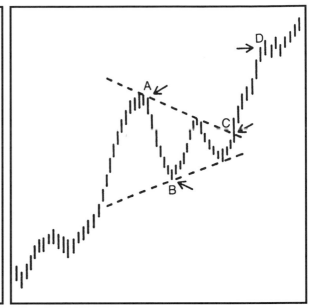

| **Flag** | **Triangle (Symmetrical)** |

Pennants and Flags—The measuring characteristic of these Continuation patterns is a move from the last test of the lower boundary (long) or upper boundary (short) equal to the pole-rally. Graphically, the rally from A to B is repeated from C to D. Generally, these patterns "fly at half mast" and the leg-in will equal the leg-out.

Triangles—When a stock breaks out of a Symmetrical Triangle (either up or down), the ensuing move should carry at least as far as the height of the Triangle as measured along its first Reaction. In the illustration, the measurement is taken from A to B, and the objective plotted by C to D. Right Triangles are measured in similar fashion.

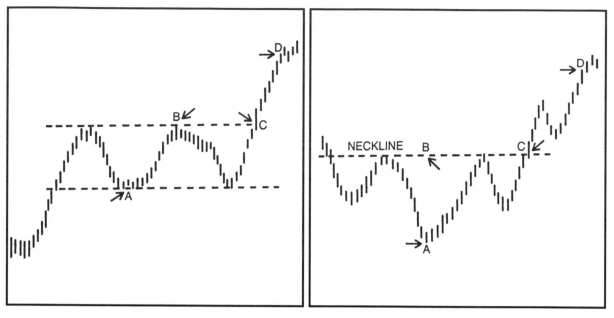

Rectangle

Head-and-Shoulders Bottom

Rectangles—The minimum expectation of breakout C to D (up or down) is equal to the height A to B of the formation.

Head-and-Shoulders Tops/Bottoms—The Head-and-Shoulders formation is one of the most reliable measuring patterns. On either a Top or Bottom the interim target, once the Neckline is penetrated, is the distance from the Top (or Bottom) of the Head to the level of the Neckline directly below (above) the Head. In the illustration, A to B is the measurement and C to D the objective.

Analyzing Bar Charts for Profit

Index

A

Acquisitions, 137
Advanced Micro Devices Inc., 50, 54
Alleghany Corporation, 97
Allied Stores, 140, 141-142
AMAX Inc., 60, 173, 174
Amerada Hess, 137, 141-142
American Brands Inc., 65
American Broadcasting Company, 137
American Express, 97
American Financial Corporation, 141
American Medical Intl., 174
American Sterilizer, 92
Anheuser Busch, 92
ARKLA, 92
Arvin Industries, 56
Asset Allocation, 83
AT&T, 184
Atlantic Richfield, 92
Averaging Cost, 139, 182
AVX Corporation, 92

B

Bally Manufacturing Corporation, 64
BankAmerica, 53, 54
Barron's, 134, 141-142, 145
Blue Chips, 1, 184
Bottom, 8, 57, 64, 66, 81, 96, 97, 98, 113,
135-136, 147, 159, 161, 174, 179
    Dormant, 190, 212
    Double Formation, 52, 60, 61, 113, 136, 147
    Head and Shoulders, 64, 67, 69, 161-162,
    163, 173-174, 194, 208, 211, 218
    Major, 69, 120
    Pendant, 69
    Rounding, 65, 163, 164, 190, 203, 204, 212
    Triple, 208, 211
Bowl, 70, 163, 190, 203, 204

    Inverted, 70, 163, 203,
Breakout, 8, 43, 44, 45, 52, 53, 55, 56, 58, 59, 61,
69, 76, 103, 111, 112, 161, 164, 175, 176, 177,
182, 184, 189, 190, 191, 192, 193, 194, 195, 201
    Downside, 58, 174, 191, 201, 207
    Rectangle, 56
    Triangle, 173, 203
    Upside, 103, 162, 174, 191, 201, 207

C

Calls, Covered, 97, 108
CAP, Inc., 149
Capital Cities Communication, 137
Central Soya, 137
Channel, 49, 107, 186
    Ascending Trend, 181
    Descending Trend, 188
    Downtrend, 73, 168
    Horizontal Trend, 44, 53, 53, 195
    Sideways, 73
    Trend, 40, 72, 73, 207
    Uptrend, 73, 159, 168, 179, 182
"Channeling," 7
Chart, 38, 40, 42, 43, 186
    Bar, 9-12, 183
    Construction of, 26
    Daily, 26, 69, 74, 87, 88, 136, 144, 168, 183
    Hourly, 183
    Logarithmic Scale, 26-28, 40, 48, 49
    Long-Term, 87-88, 140, 165
    Monthly, 74, 87, 168, 177, 183
    Predictive Value, 11-13
    Price Scale, 26, 29, 31-31, 181
    Time Scale, 26, 32-33
    Use of, 25, 41-42
    Volume Scale, 33, 181
    Weekly, 74, 87, 165, 177, 179, 183
Cities Service, 92
Comdisco Inc., 59
Community Psychiatric Centers, 162
Computervision, 135
Confirmation, 2, 3, 54, 69, 97, 113, 120, 159,
162, 163, 164, 176, 177, 187, 189, 189, 194, 199
Congestion Formation, 75, 76, 79, 187, 193, 206

Consolidated Edison, 80
Consolidation Pattern, 44, 51, 53, 55, 56, 59, 60, 62, 75, 103, 161, 162, 163, 167, 186, 188
    Head-and-Shoulders, 216
Continuation Pattern, 2, 3, 17, 51, 52, 53, 54, 56, 62, 81, 87, 103, 112, 161, 162, 166, 174, 175, 188, 189, 193, 194, 202, 206, 217
Contrarian Investment Strategy, 171
Copper, 115, 116
Correction, 48, 51, 56, 163, 164, 186, 188
Cradle point, 55, 188
Cray Research Inc., 70
Currency, 117, 179-180

D

Data General, 135
Decline, 55, 161
Delta Airlines, 113
Demand, 175, 188
Deutsche Mark, 179-180
Diamond, 189, 199, 215
Dillard Department Stores Inc., 67
Divergence, 187, 189
Diversification, 83, 84, 93, 132, 157, 190
Dow Jones Averages, 2, 3
Dow Jones Industrial Average, 95, 100, 117, 147-148, 149, 155, 167-168, 169, 177-178, 187, 191
Dow Theory, 1, 2, 3, 187, 188, 197
Dow, Charles H., 1, 39, 66, 191, 200
Downtrend, 4, 5, 6, 7, 50, 52, 54, 55, 56, 69, 97, 113, 119, 166, 176
    Major, 53, 66
Dreman, David, 171

E

Eagle Picher Industries, 44
Edwards, Robert D., 17, 55
Electronics Corporation of America, 140
Elliott Wave Theorist, The, 133, 134
Elliott Wave Theory, 133-134
End Run, 55, 59
Ex-Dividends, Charting of, 34, 192

F

Fan Lines, 120, 193, 211
Fedders USA Inc., 58
Financial Management's 1977 Study of Earnings forecasts on 92 NYSE Listed Companies, From 1972-1976, 172
Firestone Tire and Rubber, 164
Flag, 56, 62, 161, 165, 166, 174, 193, 216, 217
    Bear, 63
    Bull, 56, 174
FMI Financial, 141
Forbes, 171
Forecasts, Market, 91-92, 109-110, 117, 121-122, 123-124, 125-126, 145-146, 149-150, 151-152, 153, 171-172
Ford Motor, 92
Fundamental Analysis, 133-134, 145-146, 168, 171-172, 194

G

Gap, 51, 62, 67, 74, 75, 79, 82, 107, 115, 137, 186, 192, 194
    Breakaway, 65, 74, 76, 79, 81, 82, 184, 196
    Common (Area, Pattern), 74, 75, 79, 82, 187
    Downside, 80
    Exhaustion, 74, 79, 81, 82, 192, 196
    Measuring, 79, 204
    Open, 78
    Reversal, 202
    Runaway (Continuation), 74, 79, 81, 192, 204
GAP, Inc., 63, 152
General Electric, 104, 184, 191
General Foods, 92
General Mills, 162
General Motors, 184
Goodrich Company, B.F., 52
Gulf & Western Industries, 129-130

H

Hamilton, Carl, 169
Hamilton, William Peter, 66

Head, Double, 69
Head-and-Shoulders Formation, 6, 66, 68, 70,
78, 111, 120, 136, 161-162, 165, 173- 174, 187,
194, 196, 199
  Complex, 70, 163, 187, 189
  Inverse, 111, 194
Hemline Barometer, 145

I

I ICA, 149
IBM, 40, 48, 119-120, 167-168, 177-178
Industrial Index, 1, 2, 3
Insider Trading, 3, 26, 38, 196
International Flavors and Fragrances, 104
Investigating Chart Patterns Using Markov
Analysis, 165
Investment Strategies, 99
Island Reversal, 81, 82, 196, 214
Island, Congestion, 82
Issues, New, 105-106

J

Japanese Yen, 179-180
John Magee Inc., 99, 152
Johnson & Johnson, 92
Journal of Commerce, The, 115

L

LeFevre, William, 99
Leverage, 132, 197
Liquidity, 84
Long Positions, 83, 92, 108, 137
Loss Limits, Predetermined, 157
Louisiana Pacific, 163

M

Magee Evaluative Index (MEI), 95, 147-148,
149, 159
Magee, John, 107, 116, 121, 126, 133, 169
Margin, 197

Market,
  Action, 3, 37-38, 40, 43, 50, 55, 69, 115-116,
  170
  Conditions, 3, 42, 87
  Bear Market, 50, 51, 56, 155, 175, 183, 189,
  200
  Bull Market, 50, 96, 99, 100, 103, 105, 118,
  177, 181, 185, 189
  Overbought, 147, 149
  Oversold, 147
Market Technicians Association of New York,
133
Markov Analysis, 166
Markov Matrix, 165
Mary Kay, 111, 112
MCA, 152
McDermott, 152
McKallip, Curtis, Jr., 165
Measuring Formula, 198
Medtronic, 92
Megaphone Pattern, 77, 203
MEI Oscillator, 113
Merger, 129
Merrill Lynch, 163
MGIC Investment, 77
Mobil Corporation, 88
Mohasco, 137
Motorola, Inc., 104
Moving Average, 49, 198, 199

N

NASDAQ National Market, 143
National Medical Enterprises, 104
NCR, 152
Neckline, 7, 61, 68, 69, 113, 189, 199, 218
  Penetration Of, 66, 67, 68, 111, 161-162,
  173-174
Neil, Humphrey B., 66
New Classics Library, 146
New York Times, The, 115, 117
Newmont Mining, 115
NLT, 92
Northern Indiana Public Service, 152

Northwest Airlines, 114
New York Stock Exchange, 99, 205

O

Order,
    Buy, 197
    Exit, 108
    Limit, 197
    Sell, 197
Oscillators, 187, 200

P

Pall Corporation, 104
Panic, 7, 118, 200, 204
    Buying, 95-96
Pattern Width, 52
Pattern, Area, 104, 181, 182, 184, 187, 188, 189, 192, 195, 202, 203
    Bearish, 57
    Bullish, 54, 57, 59
    Chart, 26, 43, 52, 57
    Takeover, 129-130, 137-138, 141-142
Penetration of Trendline, 49, 58, 61, 97, 159, 160, 168, 179, 200, 208
Pennant, 56, 62, 174, 175-176, 200, 216, 217
Pennzoil, 163
Pepsico, 149, 152
Phelps-Dodge, 115
Pitney Bowes, 104
Prechter, Robert, 133, 134, 145-146
Predictive Methods, 11-25, 89, 151
Prentice-Hall, 129-130
Price, 3, 4, 5, 6, 7, 23, 25, 26, 36, 40, 82, 83, 90, 117-118, 127, 128, 160, 171, 194, 204, 209
    Closing, 10, 183, 186
    High, 66, 74
    Low, 74, 117
    Opening, 10, 183
Probabilities, 90, 156
Pullback, 6, 48, 82, 108, 140, 162, 173, 201, 207
    Volume, 96

R

Rails, 1, 2
Rally, 55, 66, 68, 88, 96, 98, 161, 164, 188, 193, 194, 195, 196, 201
Random Walk Theory, 151-152
Reaction, 53, 55, 65, 66, 73, 82, 88, 156, 173, 188, 190, 193, 194, 195, 196, 200, 201
    Intermediate, 5
Rectangle, 6, 7, 44, 53, 54, 55, 56, 57, 68, 75, 82, 120, 136, 161, 165, 166, 173-174, 177, 195, 202, 208, 215, 218
Registered Representative, 127
Resistance Level, 6, 8, 55, 57, 81, 97, 140, 162, 179, 191, 202
Return Line, 72, 73, 188
Reversal Pattern, 51, 52, 53, 54, 55, 56, 66, 70, 75, 96, 112, 113, 115, 120, 140, 159, 161-162, 164, 185, 186, 187, 189, 190, 192, 199, 200, 202, 203, 204, 206
    One-Day, 51, 62, 79, 81, 113, 196, 205, 212, 214
    Major, 67, 81, 87, 95, 156, 163, 192, 194
    Rectangle, 113
    Spike, 97
Rukeyser, Louis, 91

S

S&P 500, 177
Santa Fe Industries, 104
Saucer, 65, 70, 163-164, 203, 204
Scallop, 65, 163, 204
Schabacker, Richard W., 62, 66
Schering-Plough, 119-120
Schlumberger, 173, 174
Securities Research, 168
Selling,
    Climax, 7, 204
    Long, 44
    Short, 39, 44, 61, 80, 92, 95, 97, 113, 140, 159, 175, 205
Sensitivity Index, 107, 205

Short Positions, 83, 108, 139
Signal, 49, 52, 58, 61, 120, 146, 160, 193
    Bullish, 98
    Buy, 87, 88, 104, 147
    Danger, 90
    Sell, 87
Skyline, 174
Spikes, 97-98, 137, 138, 141, 205
Spin-offs, 34
Split-ups, 34, 205
Sterling Drug, 140
Stock Collapse, 135-136
Stock Market Innovators Survey, 99
Stock Portfolio, Management of, 93-94
Stocks,
    Drifting, 119-120
    High-Priced, 29, 70
    Low-Priced, 29, 39, 70
    Medium-Priced, 70
    Second Phase, 103-104
Stop Order,
    Close, 156
    Progressive, 108, 201, 206
Stop Limits,
    Protective, 59, 83, 92, 96, 106, 107-108, 119, 129, 132, 140, 168, 201, 206
    Trailing Protective, 83, 103
Storage Technology, 155
Storer Communications, 137, 149
Supply, 57, 79, 175, 206
Supply and Demand, 6, 7, 75, 128
Support Level, 6, 8, 44, 53, 55, 56, 58, 59, 63, 68, 96, 97, 107, 113, 119, 120, 162, 167, 168, 179, 191, 206
Support and Resistance Levels, 7, 66, 70, 82, 87, 88, 107, 168, 173, 200

T

Tape Reading and Market Tactics, 66
Technical Analysis of Stocks and Commodities, 165
Technical Analysis of Stock Trends, 87, 97, 108, 145, 160, 161, 163, 165, 187, 196, 197, 198
Technical Analysis, 133, 135, 145, 171
Technical Analysis, Inc., 166

TEKNIPLAT Chart Paper, 2, 28-30, 31, 35, 207
Throwback, 6, 201, 207
Time, 141-142
Top Formation, 7, 8, 66, 68, 69, 70, 81, 97, 103, 174, 159, 174, 179, 190, 195
    Broadening, 185, 214
    Climactic, 186
    Double, 60, 61, 88
    Head-and-Shoulders, 7, 60, 64, 66, 67, 69, 77, 82, 161-162, 163, 173-174, 195, 213
    Major, 113, 120, 189
    Rounding, 69, 163, 214
    Triple, 208, 213
Topping Out, 4, 175
Trading,
    Intermediate, 146, 176
    Long-Term, 47
    Short-Term, 46, 47, 75, 146
Transportation Index, 2, 187, 191
Treasury Bills, 128
Trend, 2, 3, 4, 6, 17, 26, 29, 40-71, 72, 73, 82, 83, 117, 124, 127, 140, 152, 161, 165, 166, 173, 179, 207
    Bullish, 53
    Changes in, 47-48, 49, 70, 107, 124, 127, 163
    Intermediate, 5, 196, 198
    Long-Term, 87, 146
    Major, 5, 16, 17, 40, 45, 46, 48, 51, 53, 57, 66, 68, 120, 140, 196, 197
    Minor, 5
Trendline, 48-49, 53, 72-73, 103, 107, 144, 159, 160, 168, 173, 192, 203
    Ascending, 182
    Bottom, 184
    Descending, 189
    Double, 49, 191
    Downtrend, 48, 184, 188, 207
    Reversal, 97
    Sideways (Horizontal), 48, 49, 196
    Top, 184
    Uptrend, 48, 159-160, 177, 181, 182, 207
Triangle, 70, 75, 82, 165, 173-174, 175-176, 179, 181, 189
    Ascending, 6, 57, 61, 76, 175, 182, 185, 203
    Asymmetrical, 166

Descending, 6, 56, 57, 58, 68, 185, 189, 203
Inverted, 185
Right Angle, 173, 182, 217
Symmetrical, 52, 53, 55, 57, 58, 59, 75, 166, 173, 188, 189, 191, 206, 215, 217
Turn,
Major, 49, 127
Rounding, 70, 163-164
Turning Points, 2, 17, 55, 127-128, 146, 198

U

Union Carbide, 155
United Brands, 141-142
Uptrend, 4, 6, 7, 39, 48, 52, 54, 55, 56, 77, 79, 137, 159, 162, 166, 175, 188, 193
Accelerating, 103, 104
Intermediate, 103
Major, 53, 66, 68, 97, 104
Stairstep, 103, 119, 152
US Dollar, 179-180
Utilities, 43, 80, 191

V

Valley, 60, 209
Value Line Indices, 177
Volume Behavior, 118, 154

Volume Climax, 55
Volume Requirements, 175
Volume, 3, 4, 5, 10, 26, 33, 35, 40, 49, 53, 64, 65, 67, 79, 87, 90, 100, 129, 145, 161, 163, 176, 195, 208, 209
Heavy, 59, 66, 69, 81, 96, 103, 104, 111, 129, 137, 138, 140, 162, 185, 189, 194, 195
Increased, 7, 43, 44, 45, 48, 51, 52, 53, 54, 58, 60, 61, 64, 67, 68, 69, 79, 100, 137, 185, 186, 200, 204
Low, 58, 67, 68, 69, 113, 129, 136, 137, 138, 194, 195
Reduced, 48, 51, 60, 62, 63, 68, 190, 192, 193, 206
Spike, 8

W

Wall Street Journal, The, 1, 117, 125, 151, 167
"Wall Street Week", 91
Wang Labs, 111, 112, 135
Warning Signals, 49, 90, 160
Wedge, 161, 175-176, 206, 209
Falling, 54, 59, 63, 175-176, 179, 192
Rising, 63, 70, 175-176, 203, 216
Symmetrical, 165, 166
Western Union, 97
Woolworth (F.W.), 149, 152